THE FIRST RED

What Your Dashboards Aren't Telling You

Andrew Locatelli Woodcock

THE FIRST RED

What Your Dashboards Aren't Telling You

The IMIRT framework described in the appendices is real. Visit https://www.imirt.work for more information.

First published in Ireland and the UK in 2026 by IMIRT Press

ISBN: 978-1-0676467-0-7

Published by IMIRT Press

For every coach who was told the data didn't matter.

Every analyst whose report went in a drawer.

Every team that was told they weren't good enough.

And those leaders who trusted them anyway.

Contents

PART ONE: NOTEBOOKS

“Measuring everything but seeing nothing.”

Chapter 1: The Man Who Watched

"The scoreboard shows a win but Reds are compounding."

The rain came sideways at Carrickmore Town's ground, the way it always did when the wind was off the hills. It found the gaps in your collar and your convictions, forcing damp, cold fingers into both. Declan Maguire sat three rows from the back of the main stand, hood up, hands in his pockets, and watched.

Not an unusual thing in and of itself, there were three thousand other people in this ground watching the same match, the rhythm and flow, the main characters, the ball, the action.

Declan Maguire was not watching the ball, never watched the ball, because that was not what was interesting. The ball was the obvious thing, the thing three thousand people in this ground were watching, the thing the commentator on local radio was describing in that breathless way they had, as though every Tuesday night league match was a Champions League final. The ball went left, went right, went into the box, came back out. The crowd tracked it like cats watching a bird.

But Declan watched where the ball wasn't.

He watched the Carrickmore centre-forward receive a pass on the half-turn and, instead of looking for the runner breaking into the channel, hold the ball an extra second to wait for applause from a run he'd made thirty seconds ago. He watched the left-back call for the ball, not get it, call again, not get it, and then stop calling. He watched the goalkeeper organise a wall for a free kick by pointing and shouting while every outfield player looked somewhere else.

He watched two central midfielders occupy the same ten square metres for the entire first half without once speaking to each other.

And as he watched, he made marks in his notebook.

The notebook was battered, A5, spiral-bound, the cover long since lost to rain and use, held together by a red rubber band that if memory served had once been around a bunch of broccoli. Inside, the pages were dense with a shorthand that would have meant nothing to anyone who wasn't Declan Maguire, and even Declan sometimes struggled with entries from years back.

Red dots. Blue circles. Green ticks. Small arrows showing movement. Player numbers circled or crossed out. Margin notes in handwriting that got smaller and more urgent as a match went on.

Tonight, watching Carrickmore Town FC dismantle a mid-table Waterford side 3-0, the red dots were winning.

A red dot for the centre-forward's vanity. Another for the left-back who stopped asking. A third for the centre-backs who hadn't spoken to each other in twenty minutes. A fourth for the substitute who came on in the sixty-eighth minute, looked at his phone on the bench before being called, and then jogged onto the pitch for his first touch as if surprised and a little resentful at being called upon.

Carrickmore won 3-0. The crowd went home satisfied. The local radio man described it as "comprehensive" and "professional" and "another strong performance from a side going places." Tomorrow, the club's analytics dashboard would glow with green metrics: possession 64%, shots on target 11, pass completion 87%.

Declan turned to the back page of his notebook and wrote:

R: 11. B: 3.

Eleven reds. Three blues. In a match they won by three goals.

Below it, in the margin, he added: *Winning despite themselves. Won't last.*

He closed the notebook, tucked it inside his jacket, and stood. The stand was almost empty now. A few

Carrickmore staff in branded rain jackets were moving through the rows picking up coffee cups. Below, the pitch glistened under the floodlights, the groundsman already out tending to the goalmouths with the devotion of a man caring for a sick relative.

Nobody had noticed Declan arrive and nobody noticed him leave.

The drive back to Ballymore took forty minutes on roads that were either narrow, dark, or both. The car was a well-worn VW Jetta of the type that was nearly standard issue in the area and with 247,000 kilometres on the clock and a driver's window that only closed if you lifted it from the outside and as it rattled through the countryside Declan's mind did what it always did after a match and replayed it.

Not the goals. Not the saves. Not the tactical shape or the formation switches. He replayed where the ball wasn't, the *moments between*.

The Carrickmore goalkeeper, Molloy, shouting for a back-pass and getting it five seconds too late because the centre-back was looking at the manager, not the game. The number ten picking up the ball in space, scanning left, seeing the overlap, and then, instead of playing the simple ball, turning back inside to take on a man because the simple ball wouldn't make the highlights.

The manager on the touchline, Graham Welsh, arms folded, jaw set, watching all of this happen and doing nothing. Not because he didn't see it. Declan had studied Graham Welsh across a dozen matches now, and the man clearly saw what was happening. He'd shift his weight, open his mouth, take half a step forward. And stop. Every time. Something was holding Graham Welsh back, and it certainly wasn't incompetence, he had a long record as a player and coach. No, Declan believed it was *permission*.

He pulled into the driveway of a pebble-dashed bungalow on the Ardmore Road. The house was his mother's — had been his mother's — and he'd been meaning to repaint the gate since she died three years ago. The gate remained unpainted. The hedge was overgrown. The motion-sensor light had stopped working in November and he'd replaced it with a head-torch hanging from a nail by the front door.

Inside, the kitchen was warm. He'd left the heating on, which he couldn't afford, but the alternative was coming home to a cold house and a cold kitchen and the silence of a man who lived alone.

On the kitchen table: a laptop, open to a website that hadn't been updated in eight months. The website read:

IMIRT *Sports Performance Consultancy Delivering insight through behavioural observation*

Below that, a contact form. Below that, a counter showing the number of enquiries received this month.

Zero.

Beside the laptop: a stack of unopened bills. ESB, broadband, a letter from the credit union about a payment he'd missed. And a birthday card from his daughter Niamh, three weeks late, with a twenty-euro note inside and a note: *Get yourself something nice. Or pay the electric. Love you, Da. x*

He'd paid the electric.

And beside the bills, in a small velvet box that had sat on that table since his mother's funeral: a ring. Gold, thin, with a tiny emerald. Not particularly valuable in any objective sense but invaluable in every other.

Declan put the kettle on. No matter where you were in life, tea made everything better. He sat down and opened his notebook.

He turned past tonight's match and found the section he'd been building for two months: a comparison table. Two columns. Left column: *Carrickmore Town FC*. Right column: *Ballymore United.*

Under each column, rows of numbers:

	Carrickmore	Ballymore
Avg Reds per match	9.3	3.1
Avg Blues per match	2.8	6.4
Avg Greens per match	14.2	11.7

And below the table, a line that he'd written three weeks ago and underlined twice:

Outcome = Capabilities × Behaviours.

He looked at it for a long time. Then he added, in smaller writing underneath:

Carrickmore have the capabilities but not the behaviours. They haven't even seen it yet.

The kettle boiled. He made tea. He sat back down and stared at the numbers until the tea went cold, and then he made another cup and stared at them again.

Somewhere in those numbers was a truth that nobody in the professional football world was measuring. A truth that the analytics dashboards with their GPS data and sprint counts and pass-completion percentages would never capture, because they were designed to measure what a player *could do*, not how a team *chose to behave*.

Capabilities told you what was possible. Behaviours told you what was coming.

And if he was right, if the patterns in this notebook meant what he thought they meant, then Carrickmore Town FC, for all their money and talent and gleaming performance centre, were heading for something they couldn't see.

Because while the scoreboard was green his notebook was red.

DECLAN'S NOTEBOOK

Carrickmore v Waterford Utd
League of Ireland Premier Division, Matchday 24
Tue 14 Mar. Att: ~3,100. Weather: rain, wind W.

REDS (negative behavioural signals):

●●●●● ●●●●● ● Total: 11

#9: held ball for applause (2x)
#3: stopped calling after ignored
#4+#5: zero comms, 45 mins
#9: turned inside, simple ball ON (3x)
#16: checked phone before coming on
#16: jogged onto pitch — no urgency
#1: organised wall — nobody listened

BLUES (positive behavioural signals):

○○○ Total: 3

#6: covered for #3, unprompted (1x)
#8: encouraged #11 after missed chance
#7: scanned before receiving, played first-time (1x)

MARGIN NOTES:

Winning despite themselves. This can't last.

Their #9 hasn't acknowledged a teammate's goal in 3 matches. Not once. Watch this.

Welsh sees it. He starts to react every time. Then stops. Why? Who's stopping him?

R: 11 B: 3 → Score: 3-0 (won)

If their dashboards say green tomorrow, they're measuring the wrong things. Lagging, not leading. Watch this.

Chapter 2: The Draw

"To them, a warm-up. To us, a single chance."

The FAI Cup second-round draw was made on a Thursday afternoon, streamed live on the FAI website and watched by approximately nine thousand people, most of whom were refreshing their phones during work meetings. The format was unchanged since time immemorial: two former internationals at a table, a glass bowl of numbered balls, and a level of television production that, well, wasn't *quite*.

In Ballymore, five people watched.

Fr. Tommy Walsh watched on the ancient desktop computer in the parish office, the screen so old it gave everything a faint yellow tinge, as though the entire world of Irish football existed inside a nicotine stain. He had the sound off because Mrs Hennessey was on the phone in the next room complaining about the flower rota, and he'd learned long ago that Mrs Hennessey's voice carried through walls with the persistence of damp and in a battle between Mrs Hennessey and the television, there would only ever be one winner.

Ciarán Donnelly watched on his phone, in the cab of a van parked outside a building site in Dungarvan, eating a ham sandwich with one hand and clenching the other, a silent prayer. He'd scored the winner against a Dublin junior side in the first round. It had been a scrappy tap-in that he'd celebrate for the rest of his life and the thought of drawing one of the big Dublin clubs had kept him awake for three nights.

Seamus O'Donnell — Shay to everyone who knew him — didn't watch. He was teaching third-year geography when the draw was made and only learned the result from a text message sent by seventeen different people simultaneously. His phone buzzed so many times in his jacket pocket that the students thought someone must have died.

Rory Kavanagh was asleep. He'd been on a night shift rewiring a unit in Clonmel and got home at seven in the morning. He didn't learn the result until four o'clock, when he woke up to forty-three missed calls and a WhatsApp group that had generated more messages in six hours than it normally produced in a month.

And Declan Maguire, a GAA coach who wasn't even involved with Ballymore United in any capacity yet, watched from his kitchen table with the same quiet attention he brought to everything. He saw Ball 34 (Ballymore United) drawn from the bowl. He saw Ball 7 (Carrickmore Town FC) drawn after it. He saw the two former internationals exchange a glance that contained, in its brief flicker, the universal punditry assessment: *mismatch*.

He reached for his notebook. Opened it to the comparison table. Ran his finger down the columns of Reds and Blues. Stared at them, understood what they meant, knew it deep inside.

And he spoke quietly to the empty table, fingers touching the ring he wore on his left hand as if checking it was still there. “This is it, Ciara. I can feel it. We’re about to get our chance.”

In the Larkfield Holdings boardroom on Fitzwilliam Square in Dublin, all glass and oak and a view of the green that cost more per square foot than most of Ballymore’s housing stock, Mark Devlin took the call from Carrickmore’s general manager during a strategy session.

“Ballymore United,” the GM said. “Away. Second round.”

“Who?”

“Junior club. Waterford area. Beat a Dublin team in the first round, apparently.”

“Right.” Devlin glanced at his watch. “Good for community relations. Get the media team to do something — local hero angle, cup magic, whatever plays well. Tell Graham we don’t want bad optics.”

“You mean don’t embarrass them?”

"I mean don't embarrass us by only winning two-nil. Put on a show. People should see what the investment buys."

He hung up and returned to the strategy session without missing a beat. Within thirty seconds, Ballymore United had left his mind entirely, filed in the same mental category as Christmas charity matches and corporate five-a-sides: obligations that served the brand, not the sport.

He texted Graham Welsh:

Cup draw: Ballymore United (away). Junior side. Should be straightforward. Don't overdo it but don't embarrass us — good community engagement opportunity. Let's discuss team selection at the committee meeting Thursday. M.

Graham read the text on the training pitch, where he was running a defensive shape drill that nobody was paying attention to. He read it twice and glanced at the GM who was by now standing on the sidelines. And then he put his phone away and did what he always did when Mark Devlin made a football decision from a boardroom forty kilometres away and said nothing.

The Ballymore United committee convened that evening in the clubhouse, which was a generous term for a single-storey concrete building attached to the back of the community centre like an afterthought. The roof leaked in two places. The heating consisted of a storage heater from the 1990s that smelt consistently of burning dust. The trophy cabinet was a glass-fronted bookcase from a house clearance and held three cups from the 1970s, a photograph of the 1986 Munster Junior Cup semi-final team, and, inexplicably, a porcelain dog.

The committee comprised five men with a combined age of 294 and a combined budget of roughly enough to fund a season if nobody got injured, the floodlights didn't need replacing, and the pitch markings could be done by volunteers using paint left over from someone's kitchen renovation.

Paddy Joe Regan, the chairman pro tem (Fr. Tommy was the actual chairman but preferred to operate from the background), called the meeting to order by tapping his pen on the table and clearing his throat in a way that suggested he'd been smoking since birth, which wasn't far from the truth.

"Right. The draw. Youse all know. Carrickmore Town. At home. Biggest match this club has had in —"

"Ever," said Mick Feeney, the secretary.

"Certainly since '86," corrected Tommy Delaney, the treasurer, who had been the goalkeeper in '86 and thought it only right to bring it up at every opportunity.

"The problem," said Paddy Joe, "is that we don't have a manager."

The room went quiet. This was not a new problem, but the cup draw had transformed it from an embarrassment into a crisis. Damien Halpin had resigned three weeks ago after a dispute about training equipment that had escalated, in the way these things do in small clubs, from a disagreement about bibs to a fundamental philosophical rupture about the direction of the club, and from there to a resignation letter written on the back of a team sheet and pinned to the dressing room door.

"We could ask Damien back," ventured Mick.

"Damien said he wouldn't come back if we were the last club in Ireland."

"He said worse than that," Tommy added.

"So. Options." Paddy Joe looked around the table. Nobody spoke. There were no options. Ballymore was a small town and the pool of qualified football managers within driving distance who would work for nothing was, to put it precisely, empty.

From the corner of the room, where he'd been sitting so quietly that two committee members had forgotten he was there, Fr. Tommy Walsh spoke.

"Ciarán Donnelly mentioned something to me after Mass on Sunday."

The room turned to him.

“He says he knows a coach. From his GAA days up north.”

“A GAA man?” Paddy Joe’s eyebrows went up.

“A GAA man.”

“Father, with all due respect now but it’s a soccer match. Against a League of Ireland team. We need a soccer man.”

“We need a team,” said Fr. Tommy mildly. “Do we not?”

“We have a team.”

“We have fifteen men in similar-coloured jerseys. That’s not the same thing.”

Silence.

“What does this fella coach, then?” asked Tommy Delaney. “If he doesn’t coach soccer?”

“From what Ciarán tells me, he coaches how people show up. How they prepare. How they behave under pressure. How they work together.”

“That sounds like...” Mick searched for the word. “...mindfulness. Helen’s always on about it.”

“It sounds like what we need,” said Fr. Tommy. “Ciarán played under him at under-16 level. Says the man took a team of average young lads and won a county championship. Not by finding better players but by making the players he had into a team."

More silence.

"What's the worst that can happen?" Fr. Tommy asked. "We lose to Carrickmore? I'll put a word in upstairs but even so we're going to lose to Carrickmore anyway. At least we'd lose to them *together*, with someone on the sideline who knows what that means. And it might not be a total embarrassment."

Paddy Joe looked at the others. Shrugs. No better options on the table.

"Bring him in so."

Declan stood in the Ballymore United clubhouse on a wet Saturday morning, three days after the draw, and looked around with the expression of a man who was seeing not what was there but what could be.

The leaking roof. The mismatched jerseys on hooks, three slightly different shades of blue because the club couldn't afford a complete set. The pitch visible through the window, sloping noticeably from east to west, the goalposts recently repainted by someone who'd run out of white halfway through and finished in whatever was left, which appeared to be a shade an ambitious marketer might have called “bone” and no-one else would have bothered naming. Most likely it was whatever was cheapest and white-ish in O’Reardan’s on the day of need.

Ciarán was beside him. Fr. Tommy was in the corner, watching.

“The facilities are...” Ciarán started.

“Fine,” said Declan.

“I was going to say basic.”

“I’ve coached in worse.”

He walked to the wall where the team photos hung. Decades of them, faded, in cheap frames. He stopped at the most recent: fifteen men in the current blue jerseys, muddied, arms around each other, grinning. Someone had written the date on the mount: *Munster Junior Cup Quarter-Final, 2023.*

“Tell me about this photo.”

Fr. Tommy looked at it. “We lost that match. 4-1. But it was the furthest we’d been in twenty years, and the lads were... they were just delighted to be there.”

“They look like a team.”

“Couldn’t not be on a day like that, Mr Maguire.”

“And now?”

Fr. Tommy considered this.

"Well today isn't a day like that now is it? Today is a day for fifteen men who are almost a team but need the help to remember."

Declan nodded. He'd heard this about GAA teams, workplace teams, any group of people who shared a purpose but hadn't yet figured out how to share a way of being.

"I should tell you," Declan said, "I don't know the offside rule."

"I'll explain it to you on the way to training," said Fr. Tommy.

"I'm serious, Father. I've watched the sport. I understand the principles. But I can't coach formations, or set pieces, or positional play. I'm a GAA man. If you're looking for someone to teach these lads how to play soccer, I'm not your man."

"And what would you teach them?"

Declan looked at the photo again. The arms around each other. The grins.

"How to be that," he said. "Every match. Not just when they're winning. Not just when the occasion lifts them. Every time they walk on a pitch."

Fr. Tommy looked at Ciarán. Ciarán nodded.

"You'll take it, then?" said Fr. Tommy.

"The pay is..."

"A nice round number, Mr. Maguire. Zero, to be precise."

"Right." A pause. "And the committee?"

"The committee will do what the committee does. But I'll make sure they leave you alone."

"Then I'll take it," said Declan.

Fr. Tommy extended his hand and Declan shook it. The deal was done.

Chapter 3: Performance

"Green is the most dangerous colour."

The Larkfield Performance Centre was three years old and already featured in an architecture magazine. It dominated Carrickmore's training complex, a glass-and-chrome statement of intent: two full-sized pitches (one with undersoil heating), a covered warm-up area, a gymnasium with equipment that wouldn't have been out of place at an Olympic training facility, and, inside the main building, an analytics suite, recovery room, canteen with a nutritionist-approved menu, and boardroom with a huge screen that was currently displaying the Larkfield Holdings logo in slow rotation, a corporate screensaver for people who'd confused football and finance.

Roberta Berbenni arrived at 7:45, fifteen minutes before the morning briefing, as she always did. She liked the quiet of the analytics suite before anyone else arrived, the hum and glow, the pure and peaceful world of data before it collided with people who didn't want to hear what it had to say.

She set her coffee on the desk (her own mug, brought from home, because the Larkfield-branded ones were too large and made her feel like she was drinking from a bucket) and caught herself wondering why it was apparently so hard to make a decent

Italian coffee and smiled ruefully: and the pasta's not like mamma's either! She opened the dashboard.

The dashboard was her creation and it was *beautiful*. Three years of iteration had produced something that could tell you, at a glance, exactly how every player in the Carrickmore Town squad was performing across forty-seven individual metrics. GPS load. Sprint count. Distance covered. High-intensity running minutes. Heart rate zones. Sleep quality (from the wearable trackers that the players were contractually obligated to wear). Pass completion. Shot accuracy. Tackle success rate. Forty-seven metrics, each with a traffic-light indicator: red, amber, or green.

And this morning, as most mornings, the dashboard was overwhelmingly green.

Roberta stared at it and knew, knew that the most complete picture in the world was still a picture, and that what mattered was happening outside the frame. She could feel her unease growing. *What if we've just optimised our processes for producing green signals?* she thought.

The morning briefing started at 8:00 and was attended by Graham Welsh, his assistant coach, the fitness coach, the goalkeeping coach, Roberta, and, via a video link from Dublin that was always slightly out of sync and occasionally froze entirely, Mark Devlin.

Graham ran through the week's schedule. Training today and Thursday, recovery session Wednesday, travel to Ballymore on Friday for the cup match Saturday.

"Team selection," said Devlin's face, slightly pixelated, from the screen. "Thoughts?"

"I'd go strong," said Graham. "Make a statement."

"Agreed. But rest Hennessey, his GPS load is trending high. And give young Mulligan some minutes. The kid needs exposure."

Graham paused. He'd been planning to start Hennessey, whose experience would be useful in an away match at a difficult ground. But Devlin was reading the GPS data, and the GPS data said Hennessey had run a lot recently, and to Mark Devlin, data points were commands not suggestions.

"Mark, Hennessey's our most experienced —"

"The data says rest him." He paused and then spoke more gently. "This is the same conversation we had last season, remember? I insisted on resting a player based on GPS load and straight after that match he injured himself in training. It would have been a lot worse if we'd played him. You agreed afterwards it was the right call, didn't you?" Graham nodded because in retrospect it had been the right call, even if it was his right to make the call. "I think we're heading into the same territory again. You agree that we will need him for Drogheda?" Another nod. "So the data shows that we *need* to rest him. This is Ballymore, Graham. We could play the under-19s. We could play the under-12s, it's not going to make much difference. We're building a world-class team here to showcase what Irish football can do and we have to plan games and even *seasons* ahead."

Graham looked at the table. Then at the screen. Then at the table again. He could feel the words building on his tongue, forcing their way out against a dam that was close to breaking: that's as may be, Mark, but it's *my* call.

He opened his mouth and said: "Fine."

"Good. What else?"

Roberta saw her opening. "I have the weekly cohesion update."

"Go ahead."

She shared her screen. A graph appeared: *Team Communication Frequency — Match Actions (Verbal + Non-Verbal), Last 8 Weeks.*

The line was trending down, tilted like Ballymore's pitch. The line looked like a flight of stairs: sharp drops, brief plateaus where you thought it might recover, then another drop.

"Communication actions during matches are down over forty percent over eight weeks," Roberta said. "That includes verbal calls, directional pointing, eye contact before passing, and acknowledgement of teammates' contributions."

"What's driving it?" Graham asked. He was leaning forward. He already knew the answer, but he wanted it on the record.

"Several factors. Player-to-player relationships have fragmented — the squad has formed three distinct sub-groups based on social connection, and cross-group communication is significantly lower than within-group. The forward line is particularly isolated. Fitzpatrick hasn't completed a pass to another forward in open play in three matches."

The room was quiet.

"And this matters because?" Devlin asked from the screen.

"Because our research shows that communication frequency is a leading indicator of defensive organisation, transition speed, and set-piece effectiveness. When communication drops, the outcomes follow. Usually with a two-to-three-week lag."

"And our results in the last three weeks?"

"Won two, drew one."

"So the results don't support the concern."

Roberta took a breath. “Well, they’re a *leading* indicator, they show first. I’m concerned that the results just haven’t caught up yet. And by the time they do reflect the communication drop, it will be much harder to correct.”

Devlin looked at something off-camera. His phone, probably. “Roberta, this is good work but I’d like more of a focus on hard data points going forwards, please. These metrics are *key*; we can see everything, optimise everything. They’ve not led us wrong and we just need to keep trusting them. File it with the weekly report. Graham, keep an eye on it, please.”

File it. Keep an eye on it. Always the same response to every piece of analysis that didn’t align with the narrative he’d already decided on, which was that Carrickmore Town were performing well, the investment was paying off, and the data — his data, on his dashboard, in his performance centre — confirmed it.

And, to be fair to Devlin, the data did indeed confirm it, the decisions to date were sound and backed by the data. The investments were paying off. The results were excellent. The team were at their technical peak. But this was part of what was driving her unease. The lagging indicators were starting to disagree with the leading ones and the leading ones would always win that argument. She had a growing sense that the dashboard was obscuring something important that they were failing to understand.

The meeting moved on to sponsorship activations for the cup match. Devlin wanted the players in the new training tops during the warm-up. He wanted a photographer from the Larkfield marketing team. He wanted the social media team to produce "behind the scenes" content.

Graham sat through this and said nothing. Roberta noticed his jaw working, the small, rhythmic clenching that she'd come to recognise as Graham Welsh's only visible expression of what she suspected was a vast and constantly replenishing reservoir of frustration.

Training that morning was technically excellent.

But the players arrived in ones and twos, never together. Roberta noticed this, because she noticed everything. The Irish players clustered by the coffee machine. The two foreign signings, who spoke limited English and had been provided with no language support because nobody had thought to ask, sat at a separate table. The academy graduates, still young enough to be intimidated by the seniors, occupied a third space near the door, ready to leave the room quickly if the dynamic shifted.

Three disparate groups. All wearing the same kit and training in the same centre with the same coach but looking less and less like a team.

On the training pitch, the session ran according to Graham's plan, with suitable suggestions and input from the committee after Thursday's meeting. Suggestions which had added a drone filming requirement (Devlin wanted footage for a corporate presentation) and removed the small-sided game Graham had wanted to end with (the fitness coach felt it was "unnecessary additional load" based on the GPS data).

Conor Fitzpatrick arrived fourteen minutes late. He walked onto the pitch adjusting his headband, gave Graham a wave that could have been an apology or a greeting, and slotted into the session as though time-keeping was a concept that applied to other people.

Nobody said anything. Nobody had said anything the last eight times this had happened, because Conor had scored twelve goals this season and as Mark Devlin liked to remark, Carrickmore were in the business of scoring goals. And goals clearly bought immunity from accountability.

Roberta, watching from the touchline with her tablet, made a note: *CF late again. No consequence. No acknowledgement from teammates. How do you build standards when your best player is exempt from them?*

She watched the tactical drill: a structured attacking pattern, rehearsed repeatedly, designed to create overloads on the left wing. It was well-conceived. The players executed it competently. The GPS data would show good intensity, good distance covered, good sprint numbers.

But Roberta wasn't watching the pattern. She was watching what happened *between* the repetitions. The moments when the drill paused and the players reset. She was in fact watching where the ball wasn't.

And nobody talked. In the spaces between the structure, when the players were briefly left to organise themselves, they stood in their three groups and waited to be told what to do next. No one asked a question. No one offered a suggestion. No one said, "What if we tried it this way?"

Graham ran the session for ninety minutes. He spoke for approximately eighty of them. The players listened, nodded, executed, and contributed nothing.

At one point, a young midfielder — Liam Hegarty, a squad player on the fringe — started to raise his hand during a water break, as though he had a thought about the drill. Graham saw it and turned towards him. From the far touchline, Devlin's voice came through the walkie-talkie he insisted Graham carry: “Graham, let’s stick to the plan. Clock’s ticking.”

Hegarty lowered his hand. His thought, whatever it was, died unspoken.

After training, in the analytics suite, Roberta processed the data. GPS loads: on target. Sprint counts: within range. Heart rate recovery: normal. The dashboard refreshed. Green, green, green.

She opened a new document and typed a title she already knew nobody would read:

Behavioural Cohesion Assessment — Week 24

She typed for an hour. She documented the communication decline, the sub-group fragmentation, the lateness culture, the absence of player-initiated dialogue. She attached data, drew conclusions, made recommendations.

She saved the document, attached it to an email addressed to Devlin, Graham, and the two board members on the Football Operations Committee, and pressed send.

Then she sat back and looked at the dashboard. All green.

She thought about a phrase she’d heard at a sports analytics conference two years ago, from a presenter whose name she’d forgotten, Kieran something-

or-other: *The most dangerous colour in business isn't red. It's green. Because green tells you everything is fine. And sometimes, everything is not fine. Sometimes, green is just the colour of not looking hard enough.*

Toxic green, the presenter had called it.

Roberta looked at her dashboard and thought: *This is the greenest thing I've ever seen. What are we missing?*

Graham Welsh's office was a small room at the back of the performance centre, wedged between the recovery room and a storage cupboard. It was the only space in the building that didn't feel like it had been designed by an architect. Largely because it hadn't. It had been an afterthought, added when someone realised the head coach might need somewhere to sit that wasn't the canteen.

He was there at 9 PM, long after everyone had left, watching match footage on his laptop. Not Carrickmore's footage. Ballymore United's.

He'd requested Ballymore's most recent game from the Munster Football Association archive. Poor quality, filmed from a single camera angle at the halfway line, but enough.

He watched it twice.

The first time, he watched the football. It was journeyman. Honest, hard-working, limited technically. A couple of players had something, the big centre-forward was lively, and a midfielder he didn't recognise moved with an intelligence that seemed out of place at this level. But nothing that would trouble a League of Ireland defence.

The second time, he watched the spaces, watched where the ball wasn't. He watched the communication, the body language, the way players responded to each other. They moved together, they looked like a team. Amateurs, certainly and the gaps in fitness and technique were obvious but there was a cohesion to their movement that he recognised. Players were talking, constantly. After every passage of play, someone was organising, pointing, adjusting. When the centre-back made an error, the goalkeeper immediately communicated, not criticism, but direction. When the striker missed a chance, the nearest teammate clapped his back. These were small things. Individually meaningless. Collectively somewhat troubling.

Graham paused the footage. Sat back. Rubbed his eyes.

He opened a browser and searched: *Ballymore United new manager.* Nothing. A Junior club appointment wouldn't make the news. He tried social media. Found the club's Facebook page, which had

340 followers and mostly posted about lotto results and fixture changes. Nothing about a new coach.

He searched: *Ballymore United FAI Cup*. Found a match report from a local Waterford news site. Four paragraphs. The last line read: *Ballymore will face League of Ireland Premier Division side Carrickmore Town FC in the second round. The match is expected to be played at Ballymore's ground, with a date to be confirmed.*

No mention of a manager. No mention of anything that would explain the cohesion he'd seen on that footage.

He closed the laptop. Picked up his phone. Texted Devlin:

Mark, watched Ballymore footage. They're well drilled. More than you'd expect for a Junior side. Suggest we prepare properly for this.

The reply came almost immediately:

Graham, they're a Junior team with a budget you'd spend on protein powder. We have the better players! Relax. See you at Thursday's committee meeting. M.

Graham put his phone face-down on the desk and stared at the wall. On the wall was a framed photograph from his own playing days — a league title win, thirteen years ago, a different club, a different life. In the photograph, he was lifting the trophy with one hand and pointing at a teammate with the other. The teammate was the man who'd scored the winning goal. Graham had made the pass.

He looked at the photograph for a long time. Then he looked at the dark, empty training pitch through his window. Then he went home.

CARRICKMORE TOWN FC

Performance Dashboard — Week 24

Overall Status: ● **GREEN**

● GPS Load Compliance	94%
● Sprint Count (avg)	+3%
● Pass Completion	87.2%
● Shot Accuracy	41%
● Tackle Success Rate	72%
● Results (trailing 5)	W W D W W

Attachment:
Behavioural_Cohesion_Wk24.pdf

Status: **UNREAD**

Key finding:

Communication frequency down 41% over 8 weeks.

Cross-group interaction at season low. Forward line isolated.

Recommendation:

Structured team-bonding sessions.
Review individual incentives.
Empower coaching staff to address behaviours directly.

Chapter 4: Metrics

"I don't predict what will happen. I watch what already is."

Aoife Brennan had been going out with Ciarán Donnelly for two years. And in those two years, she must have heard the name Declan Maguire at least four hundred times. Declan said this. Declan taught us that. Declan would say you should look at it this way. She'd formed a mental picture of the man long before she met him: part GAA sage, part mystic, and, she suspected, part figment of Ciarán's nostalgic imagination, the way people sometimes turned ordinary coaches from their youth into legends through distance and fondness. She also half-expected him to wear some sort of mystic robe.

But the actual Declan Maguire, sitting across from her at his kitchen table on a Thursday evening in late March, was not particularly mystic nor wearing a robe. In fact, he didn't really meet expectations at all now she was up close to him. He was smaller than she'd imagined, for a start, and thin, more from forgetting to eat rather than choosing not to. His hair was grey and desperately needed cutting. His eyes were sharp. Sharp was the word that came to mind immediately: like a raptor's, taking in everything and giving away nothing. He was wearing a fleece that had seen better decades and drinking tea from a chipped mug that said *World's Best Grandad*, which he wasn't.

"Ciarán says you're a maths teacher," he said.

"Secondary school. Junior cycle, mostly. Although I'll take anything if the sub work dries up." She paused. "He says you need someone who can do numbers."

"Ideally I need someone who can tell me if I'm seeing real patterns or imagining them."

"And the difference would be..."

"Nearly ten years and hundreds of notebook pages."

He pushed a stack of notebooks across the table. There were nine of them, varying in size, colour, and state of decay. The oldest was held together with tape. The newest was the one she'd seen him carrying at the first training session she'd attended. Ciarán had dragged her along, protesting and she'd watched a man who didn't know the offside rule somehow command the attention of fifteen amateur footballers for ninety minutes without once raising his voice.

"Open any page," he said.

She opened the newest notebook to a random page. It was dense. Player numbers in circles. Small red and blue marks. Arrows. Tally marks. Annotations in handwriting that was legible in principle but cryptic in practice.

“This is...”

“My code. It’s the only way I’ve found to capture what I see in real time without taking my eyes off the pitch.”

“And what do you see?”

Declan leaned forward, with the careful intensity of someone who had been waiting to explain this to someone who might actually understand it.

“Behaviours.”

He let the word sit for a moment.

“When I watch a match, I don’t watch the ball. Everyone watches the ball. But what the ball is doing is the result of decisions that have already been made, whether the players are aware of it or not. I watch the decisions and the signals that tell you what the decision is going to be.”

Aoife said nothing. She was listening the way she listened when a student said something unexpected and interesting. “Go on.”

“Think of it like a poker tell. A player receives the ball with his back to goal. Before he turns, before he passes, before he does *anything* he has already told you what he’s going to do. Where his eyes went.

Whether his first touch was calm or hurried. Whether he scanned the pitch or looked at his feet. Whether his teammate called for the ball or stayed silent. Whether he talks to his teammates or keeps his counsel."

"And you track this during the match?"

"Yes and hence the code because there's a lot to track. I track three categories which I call Reds, Blues and Greens." He held up a finger. "So the Reds are Behavioural signals that predict negative outcomes." A second finger. "Blues are signals that predict positive outcomes." A third. "And Greens. Technically correct execution with no predictive signal either way."

"OK, so Red bad, Blue good, I get that. But what exactly are you looking for? It sounds a bit Mystic Meg if I'm honest. Give me examples, convince me!"

"OK, so a Red: a player receives the ball under pressure and, instead of playing the simple pass, tries something spectacular. That's not a technical error but a behavioural signal. It tells you he's not trusting his teammates. Or he's playing for himself. Or he's lost focus on what the team needs and substituted what *he* wants."

By this point, Aoife was reaching for a pen. Declan noticed and pushed a pad of paper towards her.

"And a Blue: let's say, after a goal is conceded, one player immediately starts organising the defence. Pointing. Talking. Directing. Again, not a technical skill but a behavioural signal. It tells you that player is focused outward, not inward. He's solving the problem, not reacting to it."

"And Green?"

"Green is a completed pass. A clearance. A save. Technically correct. Necessary. But it doesn't tell you anything about what's coming next. Greens are capabilities, they show you what a player *can do*. Reds and Blues show you how a player or team *choose to behave*. And I'm convinced that it's the choosing that decides what happens. But here's the kicker: no-one tracks or trains the Reds and Blues, only ever the Greens."

Aoife was writing quickly. She stopped and looked up. "How many matches have you tracked?"

"Two hundred odd over nine years."

"And you've done this by hand? Every match?"

"Every match."

"And you've been doing this at Carrickmore matches as well?"

Declan's expression shifted slightly, a flicker that might have been amusement. "For the last two months. Since I realised we might face them. Every other team within reach too."

"Before Ballymore were even drawn against them?"

"I don't track teams because I think I'll need to. I track teams because I need to understand. Carrickmore are interesting. They win a lot. Their capabilities are among the best in the league. But their behavioural profile is..."

He searched for the word.

"Alarming."

Aoife pulled the comparison table towards her. The one from the back of the newest notebook.

	Carrickmore (avg)	Ballymore (avg)
Reds per match	9.3	3.1
Blues per match	2.8	6.4

She let out a low whistle. "So Carrickmore produce three times our Reds and less than half our Blues."

"And they still win most of their matches. But I'm convinced they win because the capability gap between them and their opposition is so large that the behaviours don't matter — yet. They can afford nine

Reds a match because they're so much more talented than everyone they play that they win anyway."

"But..."

"But against a team that's organised, that communicates, that fights for everything and doesn't give them the space to be individually brilliant, a team that forces them to play *together* instead of side by side..."

"Then the behaviours would surface."

"Well the behaviours are already there but under that pressure I think they could be decisive. These behaviours surface every match. Nobody in Carrickmore is looking." He paused. "Or if someone's looking, they're not seeing. I can see it in the way they play the game. There's no adjustment, no correction. The data goes in and nothing comes out. They're smart and well-funded with a good coach and individually they're brilliant ... but I'm telling you now, they're optimising for the wrong things!"

Aoife stared at the comparison table. The mathematician in her wanted more data, larger samples, controlled conditions. The human in her was looking at a pattern that was too consistent to ignore.

"Let me take the notebooks home," she said. "Let me run the numbers properly. If the correlation is there, it'll show. And if it *is*..."

"Then I'm a man who can see what's coming and predict the future."

Aoife worked on the problem for the next four days.

She worked at the kitchen table in the flat she shared with Ciarán, surrounded by Declan's note-books and her own spreadsheets, transferring nine years of handwritten observations into data she could analyse. Ciarán made her tea, kept the flat quiet, and occasionally looked over her shoulder with the expression of a man watching someone de-fuse a bomb. He was a good GAA player and a com-petent footballer but this ... this was out of his league and he admired Aoife even more for it.

The dataset, once she'd cleaned it, was substantial. Two hundred and eleven matches. Each one coded with Red, Blue, and Green counts for both teams (Declan had tracked both sides in every match he attended). Match outcomes recorded. Context not-ed: weather, home/away, rivalry, importance.

She started with the simplest correlation: Reds and match outcomes.

The result made her put her pen down and stare at the wall for a full minute. What she had just learnt was that in matches where a team accumulated three or more Reds in a half, that team lost 91% of the time. Not 60%. Not 70%. Ninety-one percent.

With growing excitement, she ran the Blues: in matches where a team recorded four or more Blues before halftime, that team won 82% of the time.

OK Aoife, keep calm. She cross-referenced: in matches where one team had higher capabilities (based on league position and general assessment) but fewer Blues, the higher-capability team lost 63% of the time.

She called Declan.

"The correlation is there."

Silence on the other end.

"Declan?"

"I knew it! I could *feel* the patterns but I needed someone with better maths than mine to prove it wasn't just wishful thinking."

"That's not wishful thinking, Declan. It's the strongest correlation in the dataset. More than home advantage, league position, possession stats. The behaviours really do predict the outcome better than any other variable I can find."

More silence. Then, quietly: "Thank you, Aoife."

She paused. Something was forming in her mind, a connection to a world she knew better than GAA or soccer.

"Declan, have you heard of Expected Goals?"

"No."

"In soccer analytics, it's called xG. It's a model that calculates how many goals a team *should* score based on the quality of their chances. Not how many they actually scored but how many the data says they *should* have scored. It strips out luck and shows you the underlying performance."

"Right."

"What you've built is the same thing for behaviours. But you're not measuring what happened, you're measuring the signals that predict what's *about to* happen. I think you've built Expected Behaviours."

A long pause.

"I just watch people, Aoife. I've been watching them a long time."

"Well, your watching has produced something. Nine years of data that says behaviours predict outcomes more reliably than any technical metric."

She heard him exhale.

"Can I show you something?" she said. "Come over tomorrow evening. I want to run the Carrickmore numbers."

The next evening, Declan's comparison table was no longer a hand-drawn grid in a notebook. It was a spreadsheet on Aoife's laptop, with charts, distributions, and colour-coded heat maps that made Declan slightly uncomfortable, not because he didn't understand them, but because seeing his life's work rendered in pixels was unsettling in a way he couldn't quite place. More than once he found himself touching the ring on his hand, as if for reassurance.

"Here." Aoife pointed to a chart. "This is Carrickmore's Red count across their last twelve matches." The line was high and flat. Nine, ten, eight, eleven, nine, ten, twelve, nine, eight, ten, eleven, nine. "It's consistently high, not a single match under eight."

"And their Blues?"

"Consistently low. Average 2.8 per match. Never above five."

"Can you show me Ballymore?"

A second line appeared. Reds: low, dropping. Blues: moderate, rising. Over the last six matches since Declan had started coaching the lines were diverging. Reds down to an average of 2.1. Blues up to 7.2.

"You're changing them," Aoife said. "Whatever you're doing in training, it's showing up in the data."

Declan studied the chart. He twisted the ring on his left hand as he stared, assessing the weight of the implications.

Aoife brought the Carrickmore data back up. “But they win almost every match with those numbers. Nine Reds. Three Blues. And they win.”

“It’s because the capability gap is so big. They’re so much better than most of their opponents that the behaviours don’t bite. Not yet anyway but they will. It’s like... imagine you’re a brilliant poker player at a table of beginners. You can play badly, the worst game of your life, bad posture, obvious tells, sloppy betting ... and *still* win because the skill gap is just too large. But if you sat down at a table with decent players and played that game ...”

“You’d lose. The tells would kill you.”

“Correct. The behaviours are already there and they’d become a deciding factor. The things that didn’t matter against weak opposition would suddenly matter a great deal against someone who could actually compete.”

Declan was quiet for a moment. Then: “Can you model the match?”

“What do you mean?”

“The cup match. Carrickmore versus us. Can you use this data to forecast what might happen?” He paused. “How we could beat them?”

Aoife looked at him. “It wouldn’t be precise. The sample sizes are different, the contexts are different, there are a hundred variables I can’t control for.”

"Not precise then. Just show me if it's possible."

"Then yes. I can model it."

She paused.

"But Declan, I can already tell you what I'm going to find because we've already seen it. Assuming behaviours multiply capabilities both for better and worse as you say but they can't substitute for them. Our capabilities are significantly lower than theirs; are even exceptional behaviours enough to compensate? The multiplication still needs something to multiply."

Declan nodded. "I know. The question isn't whether we'll definitely win. The question is whether with our level of capability, we can elevate the behaviours to make it a real match instead of a walkover."

"That," said Aoife, "I can help answer."

DECLAN'S NOTEBOOK — The System

Three types of signal. Three colours.

● **RED — Predicts negative outcomes**

What to watch:

- Player stops communicating
- Head drops after a mistake
- Chooses spectacular over simple
- Argues with teammate
- Jogs when game demands sprint
- Body language closes (shoulders in, eyes down)
- Blames others verbally or with gestures

3+ Reds in a half → lose 91%

○ **BLUE — Predicts positive outcomes**

What to watch:

- Unprompted communication (calling, pointing)
- Encourages after mistake
- Covers for teammate unprompted
- Scans before receiving ball
- Plays simple when simple is right
- Body language open (chest up, eyes scanning)
- Organises after conceding (immediate response)

4+ Blues before HT → win 82%

✓ GREEN — Neutral. Capability only.

Completed pass. Clean tackle. Routine save. Shows what player CAN do. Tells you nothing about what the TEAM will do.

THE EQUATION:

Outcome = Capability × Behaviour

Behaviours are both multiplier and leading indicator.

Chapter 5: The Bet

"It's not a hunch. It's data."

Mickey Brennan's betting shop occupied a narrow shopfront on Ballymore's main street, between the pharmacy and a charity shop that had been "closing down" for six years. The shop was small, dim, and permanently tuned to Racing UK at a volume that made conversation feel like an act of determination. It smelled of newsprint, instant coffee, and that melancholy of men who spent their Tuesday afternoons studying form.

Mickey himself was behind the counter, reading the Irish Independent through glasses held together by a strip of electrical tape. He was early 50s going on 70, heavy, and in possession of a face that had seen too many losing bets to be surprised by anything, and too many winning ones to trust anyone.

He and Declan had been friends since school. They'd played minor hurling together, Mickey in goal, Declan at wing-forward, neither of them good enough for county but both of them just good enough to know the difference between good enough and great.

"Declan." Mickey looked up. "You look like a man on a mission."

"I need to place a bet."

"Then you're in the right place. What are you thinking? The 3:15 at Leopardstown? There's a horse called Wishful Thinker that I rather like."

"Not horses, Mickey." Declan sat on a stool across from the counter. "I want to bet on the cup match. Ballymore United to beat Carrickmore Town."

Mickey put down his newspaper. Took off his glasses. Looked at Declan the way you look at a friend who has just told you they're planning to swim the English Channel in January.

"You're not serious."

"But I am serious, Mickey."

"Carrickmore are a League side. Your lads are Junior. There's a gap the size of the Shannon between those two things."

"I know."

"I watched your first-round match. Spirited it was, skilful it was not."

"That's a fair assessment."

"You won by one goal against a Dublin team that, with respect, wouldn't have made Carrickmore's reserve squad."

"All true."

"And you want to put money on beating Carrickmore?"

"I do."

"And you know who owns it and how much he's spent?"

"Enough to buy half of Ballymore, I'd wager."

Mickey studied him. They'd known each other long enough that Mickey could read Declan the way Declan read players, not from the words but from the signals underneath them.

"How much?"

"Five thousand."

The silence that followed was, by Mickey Brennan's standards, extraordinary. Mickey was a man who filled silences the way weather fills the sky, constantly, reflexively, without effort. For him to go quiet required something genuinely beyond the range of his considerable experience.

"Since when have you had five grand, Dec?"

"I can get it."

Mickey's eyes went to the gold ring on Declan's hand. "Don't do that."

"I know what I'm doing."

Mickey leaned in closer. “You know what you’re *feeling*, Dec. That’s different.”

Declan considered for a moment, then reached into his jacket and took out the notebook. He opened it to the comparison table. Then to the correlation data which showed Aoife’s numbers, transcribed by hand because he wanted to see them in his own writing, in his own system, on his own pages.

“Mickey, I’m going to show you something.”

He talked for ten minutes. He explained the Reds and Blues. He showed the correlation: 91% and 82%. He showed the Carrickmore data: nine Reds per match, climbing. He showed the Ballymore data: Blues rising, Reds falling. He explained the equation, how Behaviours impacted outcomes for good or bad.

Mickey listened. He was far from a stupid man. You didn’t survive thirty years as a bookmaker by being stupid. And he could see that Declan wasn’t raving. This was structured, data- and evidence-based, methodical. But Mickey had seen methods before and he was cautious.

“So what you’re saying,” Mickey said slowly, “is that Carrickmore’s results are masking a problem that doesn’t show up on their scoreboard.”

“Their results are powered by a capability gap that covers for poor behaviours. Take the capability gap away — or narrow it — and the behaviours become the deciding factor."

"And your lot will narrow the gap?"

"My lot will compete. We'll be organised. We'll communicate. We'll fight for everything. We won't give them the space to play as individuals. And when they can't play as individuals, they'll need to play as a team. I've watched them Mickey and they don't know how. If we can hold them and then push them, their behaviours become a negative drag and our behaviours become a lift. And I believe that will be enough."

Mickey tapped the counter. "Even if that's all true — and I'm not saying it isn't — you're asking me to believe that a Junior team with a volunteer budget can beat a professional side with god-knows how much invested in them? That's pushing credulity, Declan."

"I'm asking you to believe that all that money is invested in the wrong things. They've bought capabilities. I can feel it, Mickey. They've built a system of positive reporting, little green lights that look only at the things that they want to measure. They've built a culture of invisibility. They're not looking for reds, for problems, they're looking for proof that they're right. And they're finding it! Every time they look, they're finding it. But do you know what they haven't built? They haven't built behaviours. And when the pressure comes, real pressure, from a team that truly wants this, their capabilities won't be enough to cover the gap."

"And how do you know this to sound so sure?"

"It's all in the behaviours, Mickey. Watch those and you can see the future! Or rather, the probabilities. I'm not actually certain because I can't be. That's the point. What I am certain of though is that the probability is significantly higher than the odds suggest. I'm saying the market is wrong."

Mickey put his glasses back on. Picked up a pencil. Did some mental arithmetic that, despite the modest setting, was as sharp as anything that happened on trading floors in London and New York.

"I'd give you 30 to 1. If I took the bet."

"That's the market rate?"

"Not a chance, Declan. Most books would give you 40 to 1 or higher. I'd offer 30 because 1) you've just told me you have a system to beat them and 2) you're making me worry about the consequences of losing bets. And Mickey Brennan does not like losing bets."

"Thirty to one. Five thousand." Declan did the multiplication in his head. "Hundred and fifty thousand."

"You only get that money if you win, Dec." Mickey said gently, talking to a friend not a customer. This could be the easiest five thousand he'd earned but for all his worldliness and sharpness, Mickey Brennan was Declan's friend and drew the line at taking advantage of friends. "Even if it should be 20-1 instead of 30-1, those still aren't good odds."

"It's not 20-1 Mickey, it's more like even odds." Declan paused and looked straight at his friend across the counter. His face lost some of the excitement. "And I'm already losing, Mickey. I've been losing for nine years. If I lose a car and some keepsakes this week, it's just bringing the inevitable forward. It's going to happen anyway and we both know it. I'm an unknown with a consultancy that gets no work. I am Cassandra and no-one's ever going to listen and they're not going to let a 50 year-old prove himself. But this? This is a real shot, Mickey. *The market is wrong.* It's measuring the wrong things and drawing the wrong conclusions and it's mispricing it! So, I got to thinking: what would happen if Cassandra placed a bet...? Because I'm telling you, in this I can see the future coming right down the tracks, straight at us and I'll never get an opportunity like this again. What's it the business lads say? Asymmetric opportunity with limited downside? This is it Mickey, one shot and one opportunity to make something for Niamh so she doesn't have to spend the rest of her life struggling and sending her Da money to pay his electric."

Mickey looked at the notebook. At the data. At his friend. "Do you know what I'd do, Dec? If I were betting everything?" and it was a shrewd guess from

Mickey that this bet was likely everything in the world that Declan Maguire could lay his hands on. "I'd want to maximise my return because the odds don't affect the result, *only the payout*. So I'd probably take myself into that cocky gobshite Roy Cullen in Carrickmore and take the 40-1 he'd offer me just to get one over Ballymore. That's two hundred thousand not one hundred and fifty. And if he hums and haws, I'd mention I had come to his fine establishment by way of Mickey Brennan's who didn't have the stones for it. That's what I'd do."

Mickey paused for a moment. "Especially as Mickey Brennan *doesn't* have the stones for this bet. I'm sorry Dec but if anyone can pull this off, it's you and I can't put together 150k. It'd end me. Roy though, gobshite though he is, *can* put that together. It won't ruin him but it might put some much-needed manners on him."

"It's OK, Mickey."

"I'm sorry Dec, I just can't take the risk. Can you? A man would have to be pretty sure of his ideas to do this."

"I've never been more sure of anything, Mickey. Years of watching teams. Hundreds of matches. Thousands of pages of observations. And it all comes down to the realisation that outcomes depend on behaviours; behaviours are the multiplier, not the capabilities. If I'm right, this match will prove it. If I'm wrong..."

"If you're wrong, you don't have a car. Or anything much I'm guessing."

"I already don't have much. But if I'm wrong, I don't have a life's work."

Mickey Brennan had heard a lot of things in his betting shop. Desperate things. Delusional things. And occasionally, inspired things. He looked at Declan and tried to decide which category this fell into.

"If you're certain you want to do this, get yourself into Carrickmore into Roy Cullen's shop and do *exactly* what I just told you."

Declan drove home in the dark, gripping the steering wheel a little tighter than usual. The driver's window was doing its thing and a thin stream of cold air was whistling through the gap that no amount of lifting and pressing could fully close.

The ring was still on his finger. Tomorrow, he'd take it to the pawnbrokers along with his mother's engagement ring and a few other pieces of his life. The car would go to Paddy Joe's nephew, who dealt in second-hand vehicles and would hopefully give him a fair price and not ask questions.

Five thousand euro. Every penny he could scrape together against things he couldn't afford to lose.

Was he mad?

He thought about the numbers. Ninety-one percent. Eighty-two percent. The strongest correlation in nine years of data.

He thought about Carrickmore's eleven Reds in a match they won 3-0. About a goalkeeper shouting into a void. About a star forward who hadn't acknowledged a teammate's goal in three matches. About a coach who started to react and then stopped, every time, as though an invisible hand was on his shoulder.

He thought about Aoife's voice on the phone: *The behaviours really do predict the outcome better than any other variable I can find.*

Was he mad?

No. He was betting on something that nobody else was measuring. And the odds were wrong because the market priced capabilities and ignored behaviours. The market didn't value what it couldn't see and it couldn't see because it wasn't looking. But if you could see the behaviours, really see them, the way he'd trained himself to see them over years of standing on cold sidelines with a notebook, then 30 or 40 to 1 wasn't really a gamble but a value bet.

He turned into the driveway. The headlights lit up the unpainted gate, the overgrown hedge, the head-torch on its nail by the door. He sat in the Volkswagen for a moment after switching off the engine, listening to the ticking as it cooled and the wind in the hedge and the thoughts and fears of a man who had decided to bet everything on an idea.

Then he went inside, made tea, and opened his notebook to a fresh page.

At the top, he wrote:

Six weeks to the match. The work starts now.

PART TWO: PLAYS

"Focus is a discipline, not a default."

Chapter 6: Five Lines on a Whiteboard

"When everything is priority number one, you've already lost."

Some things were already not going to plan. In the end, Paddy Joe's nephew would only give him twenty-eight hundred for the car. The rings, between them, pawned for nine hundred and fifty. Three thousand seven hundred and fifty euro. Not the five thousand he'd planned but every cent he had in the world, handed across a counter in Carrickmore to a man who couldn't believe his luck at getting one over both Ballymore and Mickey Brennan on the same day.

But other things were progressing well.

They came in ones and twos, the way amateur footballers always do, after work, after dinner, after dropping kids to training or collecting them from it. Mud on their boots from the car park because Ballymore's car park was a field with ideas above its station. Bags slung over shoulders, some proper kit bags and some Tesco bags-for-life, all of them containing boots, shin-guards, and a water bottle, and most of them containing at least one item of clothing that should have been washed three days ago.

Fifteen men and a teenager. The teenager was Niamh Maguire, Declan's daughter, nineteen years old, home from college in Limerick for the Easter break, only to find herself volunteered by her father to handle water, logistics, and anything else that needed doing. She had accepted this role with the enthusiasm of a person who had grown up in the shadow of her father's obsession and had learned to tolerate it with affection, bafflement, and the occasional sharp remark.

Declan stood in the main room of the clubhouse, beside a whiteboard that had been donated by the primary school after their Communion preparations and still bore, in the top right corner, a faint ghost of the word *Sacraments* that no amount of cleaning could remove.

"Right," he said.

The room settled. It settled faster than it would have three weeks ago, Declan noted. When he'd started, these sessions had begun with ten minutes of chat, ball-kicking, and the general milling that groups of men do when they're not yet sure what they're milling towards. Now they settled in two.

Blue. A small thing but an important signal. He made a mental mark.

"I want to talk about the cup match."

The room tightened. This was the conversation they'd been waiting for. Tactical plan. Formations. Set pieces. The serious business of preparing for the biggest match of their lives. Rory Kavanagh leaned forward in his chair, elbows on knees, ready to absorb whatever system Declan was about to unleash.

Declan picked up a marker and wrote five lines on the whiteboard.

FOCUS

SEE THE PITCH

FIND THE REDS

STACK THE ODDS

GAME MANAGEMENT

Silence. Rory looked at the whiteboard. Looked at the floor. Looked at the whiteboard again.

"Are we in the wrong room, boss? These aren't tactics," said Rory.

"No. They're not."

"And they're not formations."

"No. They're not."

"Are we going to do formations?"

"Eventually. But not from me. Shay and Ciarán will handle the shape, the positioning, the set pieces. They know more about soccer than I ever will, and they know this group. The tactical stuff is theirs and I trust them with it."

"So what's yours?"

Declan tapped the whiteboard. "This. The thing that decides whether the tactics work or don't."

Rory opened his mouth. Ciarán, sitting behind him, put a hand on his shoulder. Settling. Declan marked it in his mind: *Blue*.

"Let me explain what these are," Declan said. "Not as concepts. As specific things you'll do, specific things you'll watch for, specific ways of being on a pitch that change the outcome of a match."

He pointed to the first word.

"**Focus**. Not the motivational-poster version. Not *try hard* or *give a hundred percent* or anything else you've seen pinned to an office wall. I mean this: every training session, every match, every half, every passage of play, we focus on one thing. Not five things. Not three things. One thing."

He looked around the room. "How many of you have been in a team talk where the manager gives you ten instructions and then says, 'Right, go out and do all that'?"

Every hand went up.

"And how many of those instructions do you remember by the time you reach the pitch?"

"One. Maybe," said Shay, from the back.

"Exactly. And you end up with fifteen players each holding onto a different instruction, doing fifteen different things and calling it teamwork. Focus is about saying No. No to distractions, no to everything that isn't our one priority."

He wrote below FOCUS: *One priority. One thing. If you can't say what it is in five words, it's not a priority, it's a wish.*

"For the first twenty minutes of the cup match, our priority is this: *Stay in the game.* Not score. Not win. Stay in the game. Keep our shape. Keep talking. Don't give them anything easy. If we do that for twenty minutes, the complexion of the match changes."

"And then?" Rory again.

"And then we'll have a new priority. But we don't worry about that until we've done the first one. Remember lads: for 20 minutes, say No to anything that is not *stay in the game*. And the reason we stay in the game is because that gives us a chance to *win the game*."

The room stirred at that one. They weren't convinced, not yet anyway. They wanted it, wanted it desperately, but it still seemed impossible.

He moved to the second line.

"**See the Pitch.** Most teams play in a tunnel. They see the ball, the man in front of them, the men beside them. That's three things. The pitch has twenty-two players, a hundred thousand square metres of space, and at any given moment, eighty percent of the opportunity is in the space you're *not* looking at."

He pointed at Ciarán. "Tell them about the overhead drill."

Ciarán stood. "So. Aoife's been filming training from the clubhouse roof on her phone. Just holding it up and recording."

"We watched the footage?" Declan asked.

"We did."

"And?"

Ciarán smiled uncomfortably. "We looked like under-10s. Every one of us chasing the ball. Leaving huge spaces. Bunched up in one area of the pitch. It was..." He searched for a kind word and didn't find one. "...educational."

"That's what it looks like when we are not focussed. From above, you can see it clearly: all the effort, all the running, all the work, and none of it connected. We're going to fix that. Not with tactics but with awareness. You're going to learn to see the pitch the way Aoife's camera sees it. From above. Wide. Where the space is, not where the ball is."

Third line.

"**Find the Reds.** This is the one that will win or lose the match."

The room went still.

"I've spent twenty years watching and coaching teams and near ten years watching where the ball isn't. Tracking signals. Patterns of behaviour that tell you what's about to happen before it happens. I call the negative signals Reds. A player stops talking. A runner stops making runs. A defender's head drops after a mistake. A forward turns inside when the simple ball is on. These are Reds. And when you see them in the opposition, it means they're breaking down even when the scoreboard says otherwise. The scoreboard is always the last to know but enough Reds and you've lost the match."

He paused. "Carrickmore produce an average of nine Reds per match. Nine. That's remarkably high for a team that wins most of their games. They get away with it because they're so much more talented than everyone they play. Against us, they'll produce Reds too and probably more, because this won't be the easy match they expect. And I'm going to teach you to see them. Because when you see a Red in the opposition, you attack it. You go for the player who's stopped talking. You overload the side where the defender's head has dropped. You find the weak point that the Red has revealed, and you exploit it."

"And our own Reds?"

"We eliminate them. Or as close to zero as we can get. Every Red we produce is a moment where we've lost focus, lost composure, or lost each other. Three Reds in a half and we'll lose. That's not opinion, that's the data, your own data. Aoife's run the numbers. The correlation is 91%."

"And what's a correlation when it's at home?"

"It means that if we have 3 Reds in a half then we lose 91% of the time. That's as close to a natural law as you can get."

He let that land.

"Fourth: **Stack the Odds.** Simple idea. Every decision on the pitch has a probability. The short pass to the open man: 70% success rate. The spectacular ball over the top: 20%. The solo run through three defenders: 10%. We are going to be the team that takes the 70% option every single time. Not because we lack ambition but because we understand probability. Let Carrickmore take the 20% shot. Let them go for the spectacular. They're making an aggregate bet and, eventually, *probability will win*."

Rory shifted in his seat. He was a 20% player. Always had been. The spectacular was his currency, and the suggestion that he should cash it in for something boring felt like being asked to trade his personality for a sensible haircut.

Declan saw it. “Rory: the 70% option isn’t boring. It’s smart. And here’s the thing: when you play five 70% passes in a row, the sixth pass is the one that kills them. Because five simple passes have moved the ball fifty metres, dragged their defence out of shape, and created a gap that wasn’t there before. The spectacular pass doesn’t create the gap. The simple ones do. The spectacular pass *finishes* what the simple ones started.”

Rory said nothing. But he didn’t look away, and Declan counted that as progress.

“Last one. **Game Management.** Carrickmore will come at us hard in the first twenty minutes. They’re a professional team playing a Junior team in the cup. Their manager — or more likely, his chairman — will have told them to start fast and put the game to bed. If they score early, the conventional wisdom says the match is over.”

He shook his head.

“It’s not. If they score early and we keep our shape, keep talking, keep our composure, if we refuse to let the scoreboard dictate our behaviour, then they’ll start to wonder. And the moment a professional team starts wondering why an amateur team won’t lie down, something shifts. They speed up when they should slow down. They take risks when they should be patient. They start playing against their frustration instead of against us. And this is where we use the Reds against them because 3 or more Carrickmore Reds in a half and the odds shift in our favour."

He put the cap back on the marker.

"That's what we're going to focus on for the next six weeks. Not tactics. Not systems. Not fitness programmes. Behaviours. Behaviours are the multipliers, the things that decide whether tactics, systems, and fitness actually deliver what they're supposed to."

Silence.

Then the youngest player, a twenty-year-old named Donal who worked in the Centra and played right wing with more enthusiasm than ability, raised his hand.

"Sorry. Are we going to, like... practise football as well?"

The room laughed. Even Declan smiled.

"You already know how to play football. What you don't know yet, what none of us know yet, is how to be a team when everything is against us. That's what the next six weeks are for."

He looked at Shay, who was sitting at the back, arms folded, watching the room with the same quiet attention he brought to everything. Shay gave the smallest nod. It meant: *I've been waiting twenty years for someone to say this.*

"Questions?"

Rory: "Who picks the team?"

"I do. Based on what I see in training."

"What will you be looking for?"

"Reds and Blues, Rory. Same thing I always look for."

Rory considered this. "So if I'm brilliant but producing Reds..."

"Then you're brilliant and making the team worse. Yes."

"And if I'm average but producing Blues..."

"Then you're average and making the team better. Which is more valuable than you think."

Rory sat back. Folded his arms. He didn't like it, and he didn't pretend to. But he didn't leave, either. Declan noted both things.

"Right. Training starts in ten minutes. Shay: you and Ciarán set up the session. I want three small-sided games, five a side. One rule: before you pass, you must call the name of the person you're passing to. Not during the pass. Before. If you receive the ball without calling a name first, the ball goes to the other team."

"That's going to be chaos," said Rory.

"It's going to be exactly as chaotic as our communication currently is. The drill just makes it visible."

They filed out. Niamh, who'd been sitting on a bench by the door taking notes on her phone, caught Declan's arm.

"Da."

"Yeah?"

"That was good."

"You think?"

"I think Rory's going to be a problem."

Declan looked at her. She had his eyes, sharp, watching, taking in the signals that other people missed.

"Rory's not the problem. Rory's the test. If the system works on Rory, it works on anyone."

"And if it doesn't?"

"Then we lose to Carrickmore and I don't have a car."

"What?"

"Nothing. Come on. We've got training to run."

DECLAN'S WHITEBOARD — Session 1

1. **FOCUS**
2. **SEE THE PITCH**
3. **FIND THE REDS**
4. **STACK THE ODDS**
5. **GAME MANAGEMENT**

Match priority (first 20):

→ STAY IN THE GAME

Today's training priority:

→ COMMUNICATE BEFORE YOU PASS

Post-session notes:

Rory

Resistant but stayed. Competed hard.
Hates the calling drill. Will learn.

Shay

Already does this naturally.
20 years of instinct.
Just needed a name for it.

Ciarán

The bridge. Translates GAA to
soccer in real time. Worth his weight.

Donal (20, right wing)

Asked if we'd practise football.
Room laughed. Good sign — they're
comfortable enough to joke.

Chapter 7: Training The Right Things

"You already know how to kick a ball. Now you learn how to be a team."

Week One: Focus: The Calling Drill

It was bad, really bad. Worse than chaos, chaos laced with good intentions.

The rule was simple: call the name of the person you're passing to before you receive the ball. The execution was catastrophic. Players received the ball in silence, panicked, looked around for someone to pass to, called a name too late, and played a pass that arrived when the intended recipient had already moved. Or they called a name, received the ball, and then passed to someone entirely different because the situation had changed in the half-second between calling and receiving. Or they called a name and nobody responded because the person they called wasn't looking, wasn't listening, or was thirty metres away doing something else entirely.

Rory, predictably, was the worst. The least patient, the most resistant. The drill demanded something antithetical to his nature: it asked him to think before he acted. Rory Kavanagh's entire footballing identity was built on acting before thinking. The ball arrives, the instinct fires, the body moves. That's who he was. That's what had got him noticed at sixteen, what had made him the most exciting schoolboy player in the county, and what had got him released from a League of Ireland academy three months later when the same instinct that produced brilliant goals also produced wild tackles, arguments with referees, and a reputation for being "uncoachable."

The word still stung.

He hadn't told Declan about the academy. He hadn't told anyone except his mother and his boss at the electrical firm, who had simply said, "Sure, we need someone to finish the wiring in Cashel anyway," and had, by the simple act of not making a big deal of it, allowed Rory to move on with a version of his story that didn't include being told, at seventeen, that he wasn't worth the trouble.

The calling drill was trouble. By the third session, Rory had kicked the ball over the fence twice, sworn at himself (quietly, because Declan somehow heard everything), and walked off the pitch once. Red. Ciarán had jogged after him and walked him back without a word of admonishment, just a hand on the shoulder and a "you're grand" that meant *get back in here and keep going*. Blue.

Declan watched all of this and said nothing. If he shouted at Rory, he'd be telling the group that the coach handled problems. And the coach didn't handle problems, the team handled problems. They just needed to learn that and with Ciarán's quiet retrieval of Rory, they were starting to.

By the end of Week One, the calling drill was still messy. But it was differently messy. Players were starting to scan before receiving. A few were calling names before the ball reached them. The rhythm was emerging — scan, decide, call, receive — where before there had been only receive, panic, guess.

And Rory's turnovers, the moments where he lost the ball through rushed or selfish decisions, dropped from six per session to four. Still too many. But the direction mattered more than the absolute number and he couldn't unlearn a lifetime of behaviour in a week.

Declan's notebook: *Week 1. Communication: poor. Improvement: slight. Direction: correct. R.K. turnovers: 6, 5, 4. He's fighting it. But he's fighting it by staying, not by leaving. That tells me something.*

Week Two: Seeing the Pitch

Aoife came to training with her phone and a stepladder borrowed from the school caretaker.

She climbed onto the flat roof of the clubhouse, a manoeuvre that involved the stepladder, a prayer, and Ciarán's steadying hand, and filmed the session from directly above. The camera wasn't sophisticated. The angle wasn't perfect. But from above, the truth was impossible to ignore.

That evening, in the clubhouse, the squad watched the footage in silence.

On screen, eleven men in blue bibs occupied roughly a quarter of the available pitch. They clustered around the ball like iron filings around a magnet. When the ball moved, they moved, all of them, together, in a blue swarm that left vast empty spaces on three sides of the pitch. From above, it looked like a disease under a microscope: a dense, active infection in one area, surrounded by healthy tissue that nobody was using.

"That's us?" said Donal.

"That's us."

"It looks like under-8s."

"It looks exactly like under-8s. Because under-8s do the same thing for the same reason: everyone chases the ball because the ball feels like the most important thing on the pitch."

Declan paused the footage. Drew a circle around the cluster with his finger.

"This is what it looks like when everyone is focused on the wrong thing. Every player has decided that the ball is the priority, so every player goes to the ball. And what happens?"

"Nobody's in space," Shay said quietly.

"Nobody's in space. Which means when we win the ball, we have no options. Which means we lose it again. Which means we chase it again. It's a cycle. And it feels like hard work, because it *is* hard work, but it's work that produces nothing."

The second clip was from the same session, twenty minutes later. Same players, same pitch. But different.

The blue dots were spread wider. Still clusters, still moments of magnetic attraction to the ball, but the shape was recognisable. Players occupied spaces. Gaps between them were consistent. When the ball moved, some players moved toward it and others moved *away* from it, creating options, angles, outlets.

"What changed?" Declan asked.

"You told us to hold our positions," Rory said.

"Actually, I asked you to *see the pitch*. Holding positions was your solution. You came up with it. I just asked a question."

This was deliberate. Declan had asked, halfway through the session: *"If you could see yourselves from above, what would you change?"* The players had looked at each other. Shay had said: *"We're too close together."* And they'd adjusted. Not because Declan told them where to stand, but because they'd seen the problem and solved it themselves.

Week Three: Finding the Reds

Declan brought a laptop to training. On it, he'd loaded clips from three Carrickmore matches that he'd recorded on his phone from the stands. Poor quality. Shaky. But enough.

He sat the squad down and said: "Forget the ball. Forget the score. I want you to watch the Carrickmore players. Not what they do with the ball but what they do without it. Tell me what you see."

They watched. At first, they saw nothing. They were footballers and so their eyes tracked the ball instinctively, the way a reader's eyes track text. The ball was the sentence. Everything else was margin.

"Watch number nine," Declan said. "Conor Fitzpatrick. Ignore the ball. Just watch him."

They watched.

Slowly, things emerged.

"He doesn't track back," said Shay. Red.

"After their number seven scores, he barely celebrates. Gives him a pat on the back and walks away," observed Niamh, who was watching from the side and had no footballer's bias toward the ball. Red.

"He waves his arms a lot," Rory said. "Always wanting the ball. Even when he's in a bad position." Red.

"He hasn't passed to the left winger in twenty minutes of footage," Aoife added, checking her notes. Red.

"Good. What does all that tell you?"

A pause. Then the young defender, a quiet lad called Sean who rarely spoke in group settings: "He's playing for himself. Not for them."

"And what does that mean for us?"

Longer pause. Sean again, gaining confidence: "Let him have the ball where he can't hurt us. Out wide, deep. He'll take the shot from anywhere because he doesn't see the pass. And when he loses it, nobody will be covering because he plays alone."

Declan looked at Sean for a moment. Then at the room.

"That's what finding the Reds looks like. You've just read a professional footballer's future by watching his behaviours. Not his stats. Not his GPS data. His *behaviours*. And every single one of those signals will be there on match day. Because those lads are not having a bad day, they're living in a system that produces those behaviours."

"What do you mean, a system?" Ciarán asked. He knew the answer, he'd heard Declan talk about systems for years, but he asked because the room needed to hear it.

"I will wager that Conor Fitzpatrick has a contract with individual goal bonuses. That his annual review measures his personal stats only. That he values his social media following and knows that it is based on spectacular goals. The system around him — the incentives, the culture, the management — has optimised him for individual brilliance. It's not that he's selfish by nature, he's selfish by design. The system made him this way and he's making rational choices within it."

"So how do we exploit that?"

"By being the thing his system can't cope with: a team. Fifteen people who communicate, cover for each other, and play together. His system has taught him to beat individuals. It hasn't taught him to beat a team. Because his team isn't one even if they think they are."

Week Four: Stacking the Odds

Aoife's drill.

She set up a small-sided game with one addition: she stood on the sideline holding up laminated cards. Each card showed a number — 70%, 30%, 10% — representing the probability of success for each passing option at the moment the card was raised.

The drill was simple. When a player received the ball, Aoife held up the cards. The player had to play the option with the highest probability. Not the most exciting option. Not the option they wanted. The option the maths said was most likely to work.

It drove Rory insane.

"The 70% ball is backwards!" he protested after his third forced short pass in a row.

"The 70% ball is to Shay, who's unmarked, ten metres away, and can turn and play forward," Aoife said, with the patience of a woman who explained fractions to thirteen-year-olds for a living.

"But the through ball is on! I can see the run!"

"The through ball is the 30% option. It might work. It probably won't. And when it doesn't, we've lost the ball in their half and their centre-backs are better than ours."

Rory played the short pass. He did it with the enthusiasm of a man eating vegetables because someone had hidden his steak. Blue.

But something happened over the course of the session that Aoife hadn't entirely expected. When everyone played the 70% ball, the 70% ball stopped being boring. Simple passes accumulated into movement. Movement created space. Space created opportunities that hadn't existed three passes ago. And by the time those opportunities appeared, the final pass, the killer ball, the one that cut the defence open, wasn't a 30% gamble anymore. It was a 70% certainty, because the simple passes had done the work.

Rory scored the goal of the session from exactly this sequence. Five short passes, each one the "boring" option. The defence shifted, compressed, overloaded one side. The switch of play found Rory on the opposite flank with two metres of space and a clear sight of goal. He didn't need the spectacular. The team had created the spectacular for him.

He didn't say anything. But he looked at Aoife with an expression that might, in certain light, from a certain angle, have resembled respect.

"Like Moneyball," Donal said from the wing.

"Exactly like Moneyball," said Ciarán. "Except instead of undervaluing on-base percentage, the market is undervaluing team behaviour."

"The market being Carrickmore?" Donal asked.

"The market being everyone who thinks this match is already decided."

Week Five: Game Management: The Focus Cue

Declan pulled Rory aside after a session. It was late. The floodlights, which Ballymore did have though it could barely afford to run or maintain them, cast long shadows across the pitch. The rest of the squad had gone home.

"Sit down."

They sat on the bench by the side of the pitch. The wood was damp and cold.

"How do you feel the training's going?" Declan asked.

"Fine."

"Rory."

"It's going well. I know it's going well. I can feel it. The lads are... different. Better. Together. I know you're right about the behaviours. I can see it."

"But?"

A long pause. Rory picked at the tape on his boot.

"I'm scared I'll wreck it."

Declan said nothing. He'd learned long ago that the most powerful coaching tool was silence.

"I know myself. When the pressure comes, and I mean real pressure, not training, something happens. I lose it. I've always lost it. The academy..." He stopped. Swallowed. Thought for a moment and then appeared to make a decision. He spoke again, "I got released from a League of Ireland academy when I was seventeen. They said I was uncoachable. Three years at underage level and that was the word they used. Uncoachable."

"Were you?"

"I was seventeen and angry and nobody ever taught me how to not be angry. They taught me how to strike a ball and how to run and how to position myself. Nobody ever taught me what to do with the feeling that comes when someone fouls you, or the referee misses it, or you miss a chance you should have scored. The feeling just... took over. And by the time it passed, I'd already done whatever I was going to do." Blue.

Declan reached into his jacket. He took out a small roll of white athletic tape, the kind physios use, nothing special, and tore off a strip about 10 centimetres long.

"Put this on your wrist."

Rory looked at it. "What for?"

"It's a focus cue. When you feel the anger starting, the heat, the rush, whatever it is for you, you touch the tape. That's it. You don't have to do anything else. Just touch it."

"And that works?"

"There was a GAA goalkeeper I remember. Brilliant player, played for a small club, ended up playing NFL in America. He used two focus cues: a colour and a symbol. Before every kickout, he looked at them. Didn't think about the crowd. Didn't think about the pressure. Just the two cues. His accuracy went through the roof."

"Because of a colour?"

"Because the cue interrupts the pattern. Your anger isn't instant. It feels instant, but there's a gap between the trigger and the reaction. Half a second. Maybe less. The focus cue lives in that gap. It gives your brain something to do other than react. Touch the tape. Take three breaths. Then play."

Rory looked at the strip of tape. Then he wrapped it around his left wrist.

"Three breaths."

"Three breaths. One to feel the anger. Two to see around it. Three to see the pitch."

"And then?"

"Then you'll make a decision instead of a reaction. And the decision will be better than the reaction. Every single time."

Rory stood up. Looked at the tape on his wrist. Touched it. Took three breaths. Looked at the pitch.

"I'll try."

Blue.

AOIFE'S PHONE

Training footage analysis

WEEK 1 – Overhead view

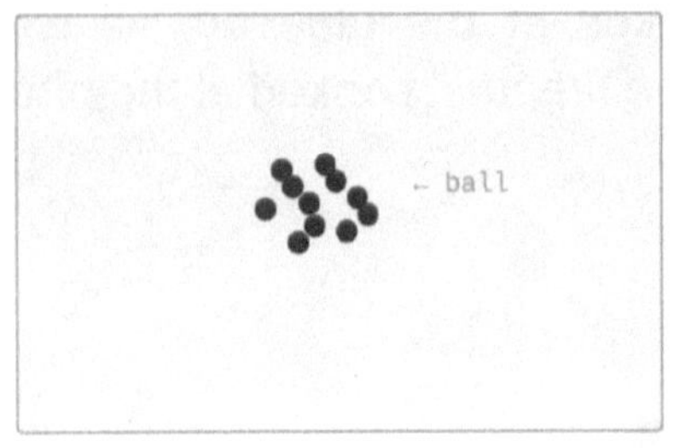

All 11 within 20m radius.

75% of pitch unused.

"Under-8s football."
– Donal

WEEK 4 – Overhead view

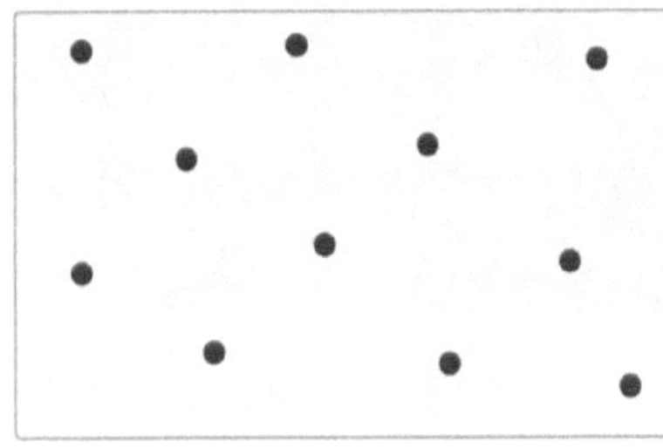

Spacing improved.

Comms up 300%

Coverage: ~60% (was ~25%).

Rory turnovers per session:

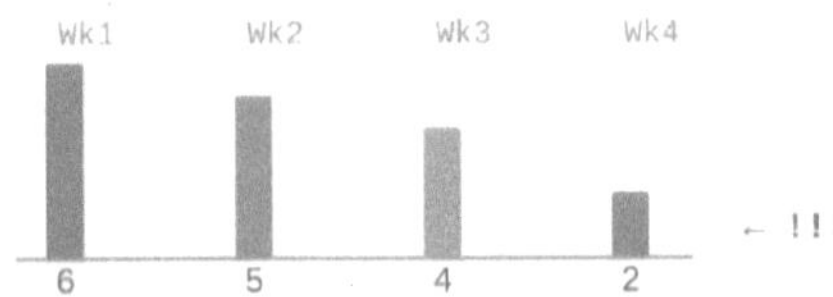

Chapter 8: Cracks in the Chrome

"We're winning, so we don't have a problem."

Three weeks before the cup match, the Carrickmore Town Football Operations Committee held its regular Thursday meeting. The meeting was, like all Carrickmore committee meetings, conducted via video link because Mark Devlin was in Dublin, board member Orla Fagan was in London visiting her daughter, and board member Paul Tierney was technically in Carrickmore but preferred to attend from his car in the training ground car park because, he said, "the Wi-Fi is better," although Roberta suspected the real reason was that Paul Tierney liked to leave meetings quickly and a car offered the most efficient exit. Red.

Graham Welsh attended from his office, which was the only room in the performance centre that reliably held a video connection without freezing, although it achieved this at the cost of making Graham's face appear slightly green, as though he were permanently on the verge of seasickness.

"Right," said Devlin. "Agenda. Cup match prep. Sponsorship activations. Any other business."

"Can I start with the cohesion report?" Roberta asked. She was in the analytics suite, her dashboard visible behind her, still green.

"Let's get through the cup match admin first. Graham: team selection?"

Graham opened his mouth and Devlin continued without pausing. Red.

"We go strong but we need to rest one or two of the regular starters. Give Mulligan and O'Brien some minutes. Good for their development. The match itself will be manageable, more of a warm-up than anything, so it's a chance to blood the younger lads in a low-pressure environment. Make them feel good with a clean win under their belts."

"I'd prefer to start our strongest eleven," Graham said. "Treat it seriously. Set the tone."

"Graham, it's a Junior team."

"It's a cup match. Away from home. At a ground we've never played at. With a slope and a crowd that'll be on top of us." Blue.

"A crowd of what? Three hundred? Four hundred?"

"A crowd that cares. You'd be surprised what that does."

Devlin smiled. It was the smile of a man who found someone else's concern charming. "Let's compromise. Start strong but make two changes: Mulligan for Hennessey, O'Brien for Keane. Gives us freshness and keeps the senior players available for Drogheda the following week."

"Mark, Hennessey is our most experienced defender. This is exactly the kind of game where —"

"The data says Hennessey's GPS load is elevated. We need him for Drogheda. That's a league match. This is a cup match against amateurs. We are the professionals and we need to start acting like it. We'll rest those who need it, blood those who need it, take the win and keep our eyes on the prize: the Drogheda match."

Graham looked at the screen. Devlin looked at something on his desk, probably his phone. The silence stretched. Red.

"Fine," said Graham. Red.

"Good man. Next: sponsorship. The marketing team want the following activations..."

What followed was twelve minutes of discussion about warm-up clothing, pitch-side photography, social media content, half-time giveaways, and whether the team bus should carry a Larkfield banner. Graham listened to none of it. He was looking at his phone, which showed a text from Roberta:

I just finished the cohesion update. It's worse. Can I present?

He replied: *I'll try to get you in.*

When the sponsorship discussion ended, Graham said: "Mark, Roberta has the updated cohesion report. Five minutes?"

Devlin looked at his watch. "Go ahead, Roberta. Quickly." Red.

Roberta shared her screen. A new chart appeared: *Player-to-Player Communication Actions — Last 12 Weeks.*

The line looked like a ski slope.

"Communication actions during matches have dropped forty-six percent over twelve weeks. That's verbal calls, directional pointing, eye contact before passing, and post-event acknowledgement. The decline is accelerating." Blue.

"Accelerating meaning..."

"Meaning the rate of decline is getting worse, not better. The last four weeks have seen the steepest drop."

"And the cause?"

"Multiple factors. The squad has fragmented into three social sub-groups with minimal cross-group interaction. I believe individual performance incentives are reinforcing solo play at the expense of team coordination. And there's a growing pattern of unresolved interpersonal conflicts that are affecting on-pitch relationships." Blue.

"Can you be specific?"

"Fitzpatrick and Rourke haven't passed to each other in open play in four matches. In training, they work on opposite sides of the pitch. The conflict from the defensive breakdown two months ago was escalated to committee, mediated by HR, and a behavioural action plan was produced. Neither player has acknowledged the action plan's existence since signing it."

"So the action plan worked?" Devlin's tone suggested he was making a joke. Roberta's expression suggested she didn't find it funny. Red.

"The action plan addressed the symptom. The cause," she pronounced it 'cows' in her Italian accent, "which is that two senior players have a fundamental disagreement about defensive responsibilities that has never been resolved *on the pitch, between them, in the moment*, is still there. Every match, the disagreement plays out in their body language, their positioning, and their refusal to communicate. It's affecting the entire defensive unit." Blue.

Devlin was checking his phone. He looked up. "Roberta, this is thorough work. Really impressive analysis. File it with the weekly report and Graham can keep an eye on it." Red.

"Mark—"

Devlin tore himself away from his phone screen. “We’re winning, Roberta. Sixth in the league. Qualified for Europe. The players are performing to their KPIs. Every metric is green across all dashboards. We measure everything and we monitor every measure. I hear what you’re saying about communication and I appreciate the diligence. I pay you to be thorough and you are very thorough. But we already track everything worth tracking, the investment in training facilities alone puts us at the top of the league and the results just don’t support the thesis of a crisis. We’re winning and we need to keep winning. What I, *we*, are building here is a genuinely top-tier football team. We’re putting Irish football on the map and proving that with the right investment, the right skills and training, the right metrics, we’re as good as anyone! You’re all doing great work and I appreciate the passion you all bring but don’t bottle it now just because the pressure’s building. Eyes on the prize, people, eyes on the prize.” Red.

“Mark, the results are flattering the dysfunction I’m seeing. The scoreboard just hasn’t caught up yet.” Blue.

“When it does, if it does, then that’s the time to act. But we don’t talk ourselves into defeat in the meantime. And we don’t waste resources in overkill against a Junior team only to trip ourselves up in Drogheda. But good talk, people, good talk.”

The meeting moved to Any Other Business, which was, as always, nothing, because nobody ever raised anything under Any Other Business because raising something under Any Other Business was, in the unwritten code of Carrickmore's committee culture, an act of borderline insubordination. Red.

After the call, Roberta sat in the analytics suite and looked at her chart. Forty-six percent decline. Twelve weeks. Accelerating. The Titanic had hit the iceberg.

Leading indicators tell you what's coming, lagging indicators tell you what happened and the committee was entranced by the green glow of the lagging indicators.

She opened a new document on her laptop and typed, just to give her frustration somewhere to go:

Performance centre measures everything a player can do. Nothing about how the team behaves together. Dashboard is green but the team is falling apart. Chairman making coaching decisions from Dublin. Graham sees it all, can't act on any of it. Most talented squad in the division. Least functional team.

Something is going to break. Don't know which match. But the numbers are screaming and nobody is listening.

She saved the document, closed the laptop and went home.

CARRICKMORE TOWN FC
Behavioural Cohesion Report

Week 26 — CONFIDENTIAL R. Berbenni

Communication:
↓ **46% over 12 weeks**

Cross-group Interaction:
SEASON LOW

Unresolved Conflicts: **3 active**

Post-concession Response:
↑ **doubled (slower)**

Key Player Relationships:

Fitzpatrick ←✗→ Rourke
0 passes in 4 matches

Molloy → Defence
calling frequency ↓ 60%

Hegarty
0 verbal contributions, 8 wks

RECOMMENDATION:

Immediate structured intervention.
Empower coaching staff to address directly. Review incentive structures.

"Discussed with board.
No action.
File with weekly report."

— M.D.

Chapter 9: The Forecast

"Behaviours don't only explain what happened. They predict what's about to."

Aoife had bought dice. Thirty of them, in fact, in five colours, from a book shop in Waterford with an extensive board game section that the shopkeeper said mostly survived on Dungeons & Dragons supplies and birthday-party desperation. She'd also bought a roll of brown paper, four coloured markers, and a ruler, because Aoife Brennan did not draw freehand. Freehand was for people who were comfortable with imprecision, and Aoife Brennan was precisely uncomfortable with imprecision.

She spread the brown paper across Declan's kitchen table, covering the bills, the laptop, and extended over both ends, giving the kitchen the appearance of a war room designed by a primary school teacher.

"Right," she said. "This is a Monte Carlo simulation."

"It's a kitchen table."

"The kitchen table is where the simulation happens. Monte Carlo is a method. You run hundreds of scenarios using random sampling based on real probabilities. Casinos use it. Finance uses it. Climate scientists use it. If it's good enough for them, it's good enough for us. And I am going to use dice."

She laid out her system. Each die represented a ten-minute segment of the match. Nine segments per match. For each segment, she rolled two dice, a blue die for Ballymore (with the score weighted toward the team's behavioural probability profile) and a red one for Carrickmore (with the score weighted toward theirs).

The weighting was crude but honest. She'd used the nine years of notebook data to calculate the probability that each team would "win" a given ten-minute segment based on their behavioural profiles, adjusted for the capability gap between them.

"Carrickmore win any given segment sixty to sixty-five percent of the time," she explained. "Because their capabilities are significantly higher than ours. But in segments where Ballymore's Blues are high and Carrickmore's Reds accumulate, the probability flips. And the data says this happens in roughly thirty-five to forty percent of segments when a team is under pressure from an organised opponent."

"Flips to what?"

"Fifty-fifty. Maybe slightly in our favour. The outcome gap narrows because the behaviour gap widens."

She rolled. Match one: Carrickmore 2-0. Match two: 1-1, extra time, Carrickmore win. Match three: 2-1 Carrickmore. Match four: 1-0 Ballymore.

Declan watched without speaking. Aoife recorded each result on the brown paper, building a distribution as she went.

She rolled a hundred matches. It took two hours, with tea breaks. By the end, the brown paper was covered in tally marks, probability curves, and colour-coded outcomes that looked, from a distance, like a slightly unhinged Pollock and, up close, like what it was: a map to the possibility of victory.

The results:

Outcome	Frequency
Carrickmore win	55
Ballymore win	36
Draw (extra time)	9

"Fifty-five to thirty-six," Declan said.

"In their favour. Yes. We lose more often than we win. The capability gap is real and the simulation respects it."

"But thirty-six percent..."

"Is much higher than anyone would give us. The bookmakers have us at thirty to one *at best*, which implies a win probability of around three percent. The behaviours push that to thirty-six percent: a twelve-fold increase."

Declan stared at the brown paper.

"Now the important part." Aoife drew a red circle around a cluster of results. "These are the thirty-six matches we win. Every single one shares two characteristics."

Declan leaned in, hand instinctively reaching for his missing ring. "Which are?"

"First: our Blues exceed four before halftime. In every win, we're communicating, covering, composing ourselves from the start. When the Blues are high early, they compound, the team builds on them, and the second half is better than the first."

"And second?"

"Carrickmore's Reds exceed three by halftime. In every scenario where we win, their behavioural signals are deteriorating under pressure. Not because we've done anything spectacular but because we've stayed in the game, stayed organised, and refused to fold. The pressure comes from our refusal to be the easy match they expected and prepared for. They're technically brilliant. Individually. But they're tactically inflexible."

She drew a second circle around a different cluster. "And here's the critical insight. In the first twenty minutes of the match, if we maintain behavioural discipline, if our Blues are on track and our Reds stay at zero, our win probability *jumps*."

"To what?"

"Fifty-four percent."

Silence.

Aoife spoke again. "You called this weeks ago, Declan. The first thing you said to the team preparing for this match was that our focus must be on staying in the game for the first twenty minutes. If we get through the first twenty minutes with our behaviours intact, we have a better than 50/50 chance. How did you know?"

"From watching where the ball isn't, Aoife." Declan paused. "I watched Carrickmore play and I could feel it, I just *knew*. They're brilliant but fragile. Survive them for twenty minutes as a team and we have a shot at winning."

"Well the maths says it's a real match. Better than a coin flip, actually. Because their behavioural decline accelerates under sustained pressure. The simulation is a little crude but it shows it clearly: once the Reds start cascading, they cascade fast. It's like a dam: it holds and holds and holds until it doesn't."

Declan sat back. He looked at the brown paper. At the dice. At the tally marks and probability curves and the two circles that contained, in their rough boundaries, the mathematical proof of something he'd spent so many years believing.

"Fifty-four percent," he said. "Not a certainty."

"Not remotely. And that's *if* we hold and *if* we can pressure them into Reds early and *if* they don't rediscover teamwork in the meantime. Otherwise we lose almost two out of three times."

"But not three out of three. Not the ninety-seven percent the bookmakers think."

"No."

"The bookmakers are pricing capability, Aoife. They're not pricing behaviour. And that's where the market is wrong." Declan reached across the table and picked up one of the blue dice. Turned it in his fingers. "This is what I've been trying to tell people for years. Behaviours are leading indicators. If you can see them, really see them, not just the ball, not just the score, but the signals underneath, then you can see the future. Not perfectly. Not exactly. But enough."

"Enough for what?"

"Enough to know that this match isn't decided. Despite what every pundit and every bookie and every comfortable person in the Carrickmore boardroom believes, it is not yet decided. And with our Blues and their Reds, we can push our chances to fifty-four percent."

A long pause.

"How much did you bet?" Aoife asked.

He told her. He didn't ask how she knew, Ballymore was a small town.

She put down her marker. Stared at him. "Declan."

"I know."

"Nearly four thousand euro on a thirty-six percent probability."

"At forty to one."

She ran the numbers in her head. "Expected value is... positive. Significantly positive. It's a rational bet if the model is correct."

"Is the model correct?"

"The model is as correct as two hundred and eleven matches of hand-collected behavioural data, a kitchen-table Monte Carlo simulation, and thirty dice can make it."

"Is that a yes?"

"It's a... it's not no."

Declan almost laughed. It was the most Aoife sentence he'd ever heard.

"Thirty-six percent," she said again. "Declan, that means we lose sixty-four percent of the time."

"I know. But we don't play a hundred times. We play once, just once. And on the day, the behaviours will decide it. Either our Blues hold and their Reds cascade, or they don't. The forecast tells us it's possible. The match will tell us if it's real."

She looked at the brown paper. At the dice. At the man sitting across from her in a fleece that had seen better decades, who had just bet nearly four thousand euros he didn't have on a mathematical model built from notebooks and coloured pens and the conviction that the thing nobody else was measuring was the thing that mattered most.

"You're either a genius or a lunatic."

"I've spent most of my life being told it's the second one."

"What if it's the first?"

"Then everything changes."

"For who?"

He looked at the IMIRT website, still open on his laptop, still showing zero enquiries.

"Maybe for everyone."

AOIFE'S FORECAST

Monte Carlo – 100 simulations

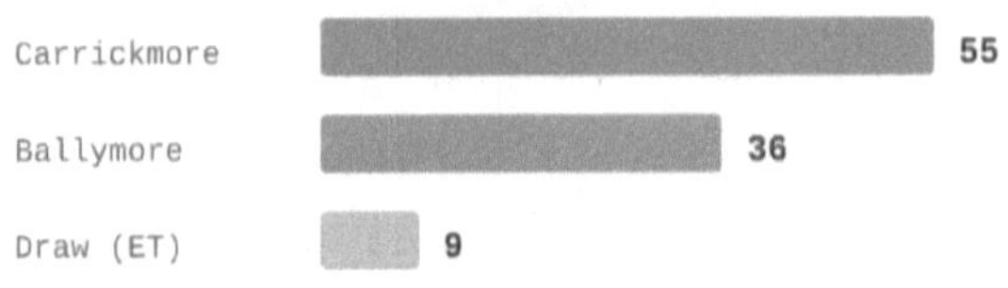

CONDITIONS FOR BALLYMORE WIN:

✓ Blues > 4 before halftime
(in ALL 36 wins)

✓ Carrickmore Reds > 3 by HT
(in ALL 36 wins)

✓ Ballymore Reds = 0 first 20 min
(in 31 of 36 wins)

CRITICAL FINDING:

If Ballymore maintain behavioural discipline for the first 20 min:

Win probability: **36% → 54%**

"The first twenty minutes decide everything. Not the football. The behaviours." – D.M.

Market odds:	**40/1 (2.5%)**
Model probability:	**36%**
Discrepancy:	**14x**

"The market prices capability.

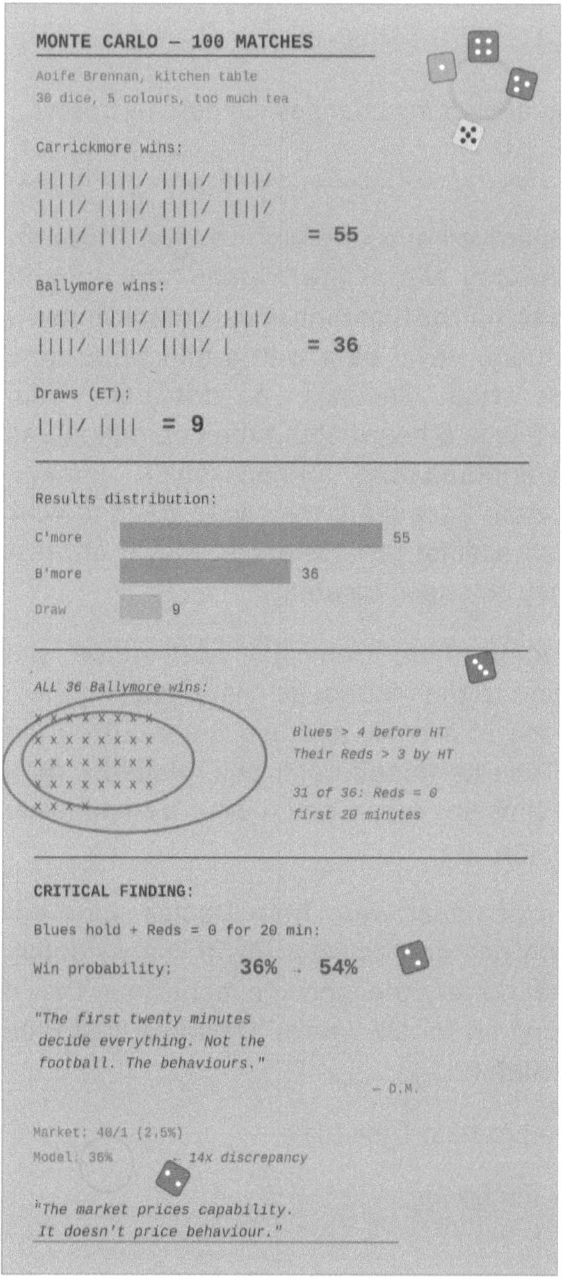

MONTE CARLO – 100 MATCHES

Aoife Brennan, kitchen table
30 dice, 5 colours, too much tea

Carrickmore wins:

```
||||/ ||||/ ||||/ ||||/
||||/ ||||/ ||||/ ||||/
||||/ ||||/ ||||/          = 55
```

Ballymore wins:

```
||||/ ||||/ ||||/ ||||/
||||/ ||||/ ||||/ |        = 36
```

Draws (ET):

```
||||/ ||||  = 9
```

Results distribution:

C'more 55
B'more 36
Draw 9

ALL 36 Ballymore wins:

```
x x x x x x x x
x x x x x x x x
x x x x x x x x
x x x x x x x x
x x x x
```

Blues > 4 before HT
Their Reds > 3 by HT

31 of 36: Reds = 0
first 20 minutes

CRITICAL FINDING:

Blues hold + Reds = 0 for 20 min:

Win probability: **36% → 54%**

"The first twenty minutes decide everything. Not the football. The behaviours."

– D.M.

Market: 40/1 (2.5%)
Model: 36% ← *14x discrepancy*

"The market prices capability. It doesn't price behaviour."

Chapter 10: Final Blue, Final Red

"Tomorrow, everything changes. Or nothing does."

The jerseys arrived at four o'clock on the Friday afternoon, the day before the match. New ones. A complete set, for the first time in Ballymore United's recent memory. Royal blue with a thin white trim. Paddy Joe had secured a donation from O'Reardan's who'd heard about the cup match and offered five hundred euro "for necessities." Jerseys, they'd decided. Because if they were going to walk onto a pitch against professionals, they'd at least look like they belonged together.

Shay collected them from the post office and brought them to the clubhouse. He unpacked them carefully, one at a time, and laid them out on the benches. Then he folded each one, placed it on a seat in the dressing room, and tucked a small piece of paper inside.

The pieces of paper were from Declan. One per player. Each one contained a single line personalised to the player, the specific behaviour they'd been working on for six weeks. Declan's final Blue before the match.

Rory: *Three breaths. Then play.*

Ciarán: *Be the bridge.*

Shay: *They follow your temperature. Set it.*

Sean (the young centre-back): *You can see what others can't. Trust it.*

Donal (right wing): *Space, not ball. Always space.*

Fifteen notes. Fifteen behaviours. One team.

Shay stood in the empty dressing room and looked at the fifteen folded jerseys and thought about the four hundred matches he'd played in this jersey, in all its previous incarnations, all the different shades of blue and all the different faces that had worn it. He'd never said anything about it, it wasn't his way, but he loved this club. Loved it in the way you love something that has been part of your life so long it's part of your identity. He was Shay O'Donnell, centre-back, Ballymore United, and tomorrow he would walk out to play against professionals, and it would be the proudest moment of his sporting life regardless of the result.

Shay turned off the light and locked the door.

In a hotel six miles away, the Carrickmore squad were checking in. Devlin had booked it ("Standards matter, set the tone.") despite Graham's argument that for a thirty-minute drive on match day, a hotel was unnecessary and possibly counterproductive.

The hotel was functional. Clean, adequate, anonymous. Business travellers used places like this and forgot them immediately. The players dispersed to their individual rooms. Graham had asked for a team room, somewhere they could eat together, watch a movie, just be in each other's company, but the hotel didn't have one available, and the idea of rearranging the schedule to accommodate a group meal hadn't occurred to Devlin when he made the booking, because group meals weren't on any dashboard.

Conor Fitzpatrick went to his room, connected to the Wi-Fi, and began editing a video for Instagram. Match-day content. Behind-the-scenes. The brand.

Dara Molloy, the goalkeeper, sat on his bed and texted his wife: *Quiet night. Nobody talking to each other. Same as always. At least the bed's comfortable.*

Paddy Rourke unpacked his bag, checked his boots, and stared at the ceiling. He'd been thinking about the Ballymore match more than he wanted to admit. He'd watched the first-round footage too, Graham had sent it to the squad WhatsApp group with a one-line message: *Worth a look.* Nobody had replied. Paddy had watched it twice but wasn't sure if anyone else had.

Graham knocked on rooms at nine o'clock for a brief team meeting. He gathered them in the hotel lobby, the closest thing to a communal space, and said what he was permitted to say, which was very little.

"Right, early start tomorrow. The bus will be here at ten. Match starts at two."

He wanted to say more. He wanted to say: *Talk to each other. Look at each other. Remember that you're a team, not a collection of individual contracts.* He wanted to say: *I've watched the opposition and they're not what you think: they're organised, they communicate, they fight for each other, and if you walk onto that pitch tomorrow thinking this is a day off, you'll be in for a shock.*

What he said was: "Get some sleep."

His final Red before the match.

Declan sat at his kitchen table. The ring box was gone, returned to the drawer empty after his trip to the pawnbrokers. The betting slip was in his jacket pocket, folded small, next to the notebook.

He called Aoife.

"Are we mad?"

"Definitely." He could hear her smile through the phone. "But the numbers say we're not wrong. That's different."

"Thirty-six percent."

"Thirty-six percent. And fifty-four if the first twenty minutes hold."

"And if they don't?"

"Then we'll have given a very good account of ourselves and you'll need to buy a bicycle."

He almost laughed.

"Get some sleep, Dec."

He couldn't.

He sat in the kitchen and looked at the notebook. At the comparison table. At the nine years of data that had led to this moment. At the equation on the back page, underlined twice.

Outcome = Capabilities × Behaviours.

Tomorrow, one of two things would happen. Either the equation would hold under the most extreme test he could imagine, a Junior team against professionals, the lowest capability against the highest, with behaviours as the only variable that gave them a chance, or it wouldn't. Tomorrow, he'd find out one way or another.

If it held, everything he'd believed was vindicated. The notebooks meant something. The years of watching meant something. IMIRT meant something.

His hand went unconsciously to the missing ring. This had to mean something, it had to.

If it didn't, the notebooks were a hobby. The years were a waste. And IMIRT was a website that nobody visited, connected to a consultancy that nobody hired, run by a man who'd bet his final few possessions on being right. And wasn't.

He closed the notebook, turned off the light and went to bed.

He didn't sleep.

In the church, Fr. Tommy Walsh lit a candle. He knelt in the front pew, in the church where he'd said Mass for thirty-two years, and he prayed. Not for victory. He was too wise and too honest to waste God's time with sporting requests.

He prayed for courage. For the boys, and they were always boys to him, even the ones pushing forty, to be brave enough to play without fear. To be themselves at their best. To walk off the pitch knowing they'd left nothing behind, knowing they had honoured the gifts and chance they had been given, heads held high.

He crossed himself. Stood. Looked at the candle.

"And if it's not too much trouble," he added quietly, "a small miracle wouldn't go amiss."

The pitch was empty. No floodlights, such as they were, Ballymore's floodlights were reserved strictly for training. The moon was behind clouds, and the pitch was visible only as a darker rectangle against the dark field around it. The white lines, freshly painted that afternoon by Tommy Delaney and his son with a line-marker older than both of them, seemed to glow faintly.

The goalposts, recently repainted (properly this time, by Rory, who'd borrowed the paint from a job he was finishing), stood at each end. The slope ran from east to west, gentle but noticeable, enough that away teams complained about it and home teams pretended it wasn't there.

The net on the far goal had a small hole near the bottom left corner that Shay had patched with cable ties. It held. It would hold tomorrow, too.

A barn owl crossed the pitch in the dark, low and silent, hunting.

Tomorrow, this rectangle of grass would hold the weight of everything Declan Maguire had ever believed, everything Mark Devlin had ever invested, and everything that fifteen men in royal blue jerseys had ever wanted to prove.

But tonight it was just a pitch. Sloped, imperfect, and waiting.

DECLAN'S PRE-MATCH NOTES

Match priority (first 20 min):
→ STAY IN THE GAME

Player focus cues:

#1	Kev (GK)	*"Talk. Always talk."*
#2	Mossy	*"Right shoulder"*
#3	Shay	*"Set the temperature"*
#4	Sean	*"Trust what you see"*
#5	Eoin	*"First pass forward"*
#6	Ciarán	*"Be the bridge"*
#7	Donal	*"Space, not ball"*
#8	Tomás	*"Simple first"*
#9	Rory	*"Three breaths."*
#10	Damo	*"Find the Red"*
#11	Jamie	*"Width. Stay wide."*

Conditions for win (Aoife):

- ✓ Blues > 4 before halftime
- ✓ Their Reds > 3 before HT
- ✓ Our Reds = 0 for first 20 min

If all three met → **54%** win

"The first twenty minutes are not about football. They're about behaviour."

PART THREE: MATCH

"The scoreboard is the last thing to change."

Chapter 11: The First Twenty Minutes

"They're scoring. But we're playing."

The morning came grey and soft, the way spring mornings do in Ireland. Not raining exactly, but not not raining either, the air thick with moisture that would find its way through any fabric not specifically designed to keep it out. A day where the sky and the ground are the same colour and the only way to tell them apart is that one of them has goalposts.

Declan was at the ground by half eight. He unlocked the community centre, put the heating on in both dressing rooms, and walked the pitch. The surface was heavy but playable. The goalmouths had been re-seeded in February and looked almost professional, which had been a source of disproportionate pride for Mickey Keane, who'd done the work himself on three consecutive Sunday mornings while his wife assumed he was at Mass.

By nine, the volunteers had arrived. Paddy Joe Regan directing traffic in a field that would serve as a car park. Fr. Tommy organising tea urns and a table of sandwiches: ham and cheese, egg and onion, all wrapped in cling film by a committee of women from the parish council who regarded feeding a crowd as a sacrament. It was the best spread Ballymore United had seen in many a long year. Niamh was running through her checklist: water bottles, ice packs, spare kit, first aid, the tactical board Declan had never once used, and a brown envelope containing the match-day notes she'd typed up from her father's notebook at midnight.

Aoife arrived at ten with a flask of coffee and a face that suggested she hadn't slept.

"I ran the model one more time last night," she said.

"And?"

"Same numbers. Thirty-six in a hundred. But when I adjusted for home advantage and crowd noise: thirty-nine."

"Better."

"Dec, thirty-nine percent still means sixty-one percent of the time we lose."

"I know what thirty-nine percent means, Aoife."

"Just making sure."

He took the coffee. Drank it looking at the pitch. Grimaced. He'd always preferred tea.

"The behaviours will tell us in the first twenty minutes. If our Blues hold and their Reds start, we're in the game. If our lads freeze and stop communicating, we're not."

"And if it's somewhere in between?" she asked.

"It usually is. That's what the second half is for."

By noon, the grass bank behind the far goal was filling. People who hadn't attended a Ballymore match in years. People who didn't particularly follow soccer. They came from the town and the townlands around it, carrying fold-up chairs and flasks and the quiet hope of people who know they're about to witness something lopsided but have come anyway because it's their town and their team and some things you show up for regardless.

Old men who remembered the club's last decent run in 1987. Young families using it as a cheap day out. Teenagers who'd come because there was literally nothing else happening in Ballymore on a Saturday afternoon, and at least this had a burger van. The burger van was run by Tommy Flanagan, who'd driven from Clonmel and was charging four euro fifty for something he described as a quarter-pounder with the defensive confidence of a man who knew nobody was going to measure the patty.

Local radio had set up a fold-out table beside the halfway line. The commentator, a man named Pearse O'Sullivan who covered everything from county finals to agricultural shows with the same breathless intensity, was testing his microphone by describing the weather to nobody in particular.

The Carrickmore bus arrived at 12:45.

It was a fifty-two-seater with tinted windows, the Larkfield Holdings logo in silver on the side, GPS tracking, on-board WiFi, and individual fold-down screens on the back of each seat. It pulled into Paddy Joe's makeshift car park and sat there for a moment, engine idling, looking faintly absurd next to a community centre, a 1997 Toyota Corolla, and a cattle trailer that someone had forgotten to move.

The players emerged in matching charcoal tracksuits with embroidered initials, sponsor logos and proper training shoes. They walked toward the dressing rooms in twos and threes, earphones in, not looking at the ground or the crowd or the town that had turned out to watch them. They moved with the unhurried confidence of men who expected to do this many times again with no particular adjustment to their routine.

In the small stand, Mark Devlin appeared in a camel-hair overcoat and polished shoes, a vision of confidence. He considered it a hallmark of his leadership that he turned up to every match regardless of personal inconvenience. He sat in the front row, placed his phone on the armrest, and opened a small leather folder containing the day's analytics: expected possession, passing accuracy benchmarks, individual performance targets for each player. He had one for every match. He kept them in a filing cabinet in his office, organised by date, and occasionally referred to them during board meetings, selectively, and to support a conclusion already reached.

Graham Welsh sat two rows behind him. He had a notepad. He did not have a leather folder. He had a team that was about to play a cup match, and a chairman who was about to watch it, and the growing certainty that the day was not going to go to plan.

Roberta Berbenni arrived separately, by car. She'd told Devlin she was "collecting performance data for the development review" but had actually come because something about this match had been nagging at her for two weeks. Something about the cohesion report she'd submitted that nobody read. Something about the way Graham's face changed every time Devlin entered a room. She found a spot at the end of the stand, opened her laptop, and tried to look like someone who was there in a professional capacity and not because of a feeling she couldn't quite name. She asked herself whether she wasn't just here to rubberneck at the disaster she thought might be about to unfold but couldn't actually give herself an honest answer.

Aoife had found Ciarán by the dressing room door, boots already on, retying laces that didn't need retying and that would have to come off again in a minute for him to get changed. His face was pale under the freckles in the way that she'd learned meant he was processing something too large for words.

"Hey."

"Hey." He didn't look up. “I feel sick, Aoife.”

She crouched beside him and put her hand over his, stopping the relacing.

"You're going to be great. All of you."

"We're going to get battered."

"Maybe. The model says probably not, but maybe." She paused. "But listen to me: whatever happens out there, I'm proud of you. What you lot have built in eight weeks ... it’s incredible, Ciarán, nothing short of incredible. I've seen what this team has become. The result today is one data point. What you've already achieved is the whole dataset."

He looked at her. She could see the fear and the hope fighting for the same space behind his eyes.

"And if we lose?"

"You’ve already won, love. All of you. And if the scoreboard says differently then it says it to a real team. Which is more than that lot’ll be able to say."

She kissed his cheek, stood, and brushed the mud off her knees.

"Now go. And pass to someone who's calling for it."

He almost smiled.

In the home dressing room, fifteen jerseys hung from fifteen hooks. The hooks were actually coat pegs screwed to a plywood board that Paddy Joe had installed in 2019 and that tilted slightly to the left, giving the room a faintly nautical quality, as though the entire building was listing.

Under each jersey, a folded note. Declan's handwriting.

The players arrived in ones and twos. Some drove together. Some walked from the town. Damo arrived on a bicycle, which raised questions about his tactical awareness of match-day preparation that nobody felt it was worth addressing at this point.

Rory was early. He sat in the corner, boots already on, staring at the wall with the fixed intensity of a man who was either deeply focused or deeply terrified and possibly both. He turned over the note under his jersey.

Three breaths. Then play.

He touched the tape on his left wrist. A single strip of white zinc oxide, wound twice. Inside, in biro that was already fading from three weeks of training, five words: *See the pitch. Play simple.*

One by one, the room filled. The noise was mostly muted, murmured conversations punctuated by the clatter of studs on the concrete floor, the snap of shin-guard straps, the occasional nervous laugh that was slightly too loud.

Shay O'Donnell was the last to change. He did everything slowly, deliberately, with the economy of movement of a man who had been doing this for eighteen years and saw no reason to rush the process simply because there were a thousand people outside and a team bus with tinted windows. He folded his clothes. Placed his phone face-down in his bag. Laced his boots with a precision that bordered on the surgical. Pulled his jersey over his head, smoothed it down, and then stood in the centre of the room and made eye contact with every player, one by one, holding each gaze for exactly as long as it took for the player to nod.

The room settled.

Ciarán, already changed and feeling a little calmer now, leaned against the doorframe and watched. He'd seen this before. Not with Shay, but with the senior players on the Ballyboden GAA team when he was sixteen. The captain who set the temperature. The player whose composure was contagious. He'd told Declan about it once, and Declan had nodded and said: "That's a Blue before a ball is kicked."

Fr. Tommy was in the corner. He wore his parish jacket and a Ballymore scarf that was older than several of the players. He said nothing. His presence was steady, warm, undemanding. He'd been the club chaplain for twenty-two years, and in that time he'd learned that what players needed before a big match was not a speech or a prayer but the quiet knowledge that someone who cared was in the room and wasn't going to ask them for anything.

Declan stood in the doorway. He waited for the silence that meant they were ready.

"One thing."

Fifteen faces.

"The first twenty minutes. Communicate. Hold shape. Stay in the game. Twenty minutes. That's all I'm asking."

"And then?" Rory asked.

"Then we'll see what happens."

A pause.

"They are better than us. You know that. I know that. Everyone in the ground knows that. They certainly know that. But they are also more fragile than they think. And in twenty minutes, if we are still in this game, they will start to discover that fragility. Our job is to be there when they do."

He looked around the room.

"Talk to each other. Everything we've trained. This is what it was for."

He stepped aside and the team walked out.

The crowd was close to a thousand. For Ballymore, this was extraordinary given their average attendance was eighty-seven, and that included Paddy Joe, who counted himself twice because he manned both turnstiles. The grass bank was packed three deep. Children sat on shoulders. Dogs that had no business at a football match wandered through the crowd with the relaxed confidence of animals who knew they wouldn't be removed because nobody wanted to be the person who caused a scene at a cup match over a Labrador.

On the far side, behind a rope line that served as the Carrickmore supporters' section, perhaps two hundred people had made the trip. They were quieter, more expectant than excited. They anticipated a win the way you anticipate a train: not with joy, but with the mild impatience of people who want to get on with the rest of their day.

Pearse O'Sullivan cleared his throat.

"Good afternoon and welcome to Ballymore Community Grounds for what promises to be an exciting second-round FAI Cup tie. Ballymore United, the local Junior side, welcome Carrickmore Town FC of the First Division, and I think it's fair to say we're all in for a treat this afternoon..."

The referee, a man from Kilkenny who had drawn the short straw and knew it, blew his whistle.

Kick-off.

Carrickmore moved the ball crisply from the start: touch, touch, switch, with the rehearsed fluency of men who trained five days a week on surfaces that didn't have drainage issues. The central midfielders exchanged passes in triangles that were geometrically pleasing and tactically devastating. Within thirty seconds, the ball was in the Ballymore half. Within sixty, it was in the box.

But nobody had made a run.

The through ball, when it came, found empty space. Conor Fitzpatrick was standing ten metres deeper than the move required, adjusting his headband, a custom-embroidered item that matched his boots and that he'd been photographed adjusting in three separate matchday programmes. The ball rolled harmlessly to a Ballymore defender. Cleared.

From the sideline, Declan's pen moved. Red dot. Carrickmore. Minute one.

The next seven minutes were one-directional. Carrickmore had seventy percent possession, and it showed. They probed left and right, switching play with diagonal balls that covered forty metres and arrived, with a precision that was a statement of dominance, exactly where they were intended. Their wingers ran at the Ballymore full-backs with the confidence of men who knew their weekly wage was more than their opponents' monthly salary.

Ballymore defended. But not desperately. Not wildly. Not with the frantic, eyes-wide scrambling of a team being overrun. They defended with shape. With communication. With the constant, deliberate chatter that Declan had drilled into them for eight weeks until it was as natural as breathing and twice as loud.

Shay, at centre-back, talked constantly.

"Sean, tuck in. Kev, drop two yards. Left shoulder, Donal, left shoulder. Good."

Ciarán, in midfield, kept appearing in the right spaces. A tap on a teammate's shoulder to shift them two metres left. A pointed finger toward a runner nobody else had seen. A word in Tommo's ear: "You're doing grand. Stay with him. I'm behind you."

Tommo stayed with him.

Minute four: Carrickmore corner. The ball swung in. Shay met it with a header that went thirty metres upfield and sideways, landing approximately where nobody was standing. But Kev was already shouting instructions for the next phase, and Rory was already sprinting into the channel. The clearance went the wrong way. The intent was right.

Blue dot. Ballymore. Blue dot. Ballymore.

Minute six: Conor Fitzpatrick received the ball on the right wing, beat the full-back with a drop of the shoulder that was genuinely world-class, and looked up to see three teammates in the box making overlapping runs. He ignored all of them and shot from a tight angle. Kev saved. Declan had shown the team video of Conor shooting from exactly that position in his last four matches. Kev knew it was coming.

Red dot. Carrickmore. The self-selection over the team option.

Minute eight. The goal.

Carrickmore's right winger, a quick, technical player named Jordan Asare who had been signed from a Dublin club for a fee that would have funded Ballymore's entire annual budget, received the ball wide and drove at Tommo. Tommo held his ground, stayed on his feet, did everything Declan had asked. Asare checked inside, accelerated past him — the pace difference was real and undeniable and no amount of effort or grit could close it — and crossed low.

It was a good cross. Accurate, paced, into the corridor between the goalkeeper and the defence where chaos lives.

Conor met the ball at the near post with a header of casual precision, redirecting it across the goalkeeper and into the bottom corner. It looked easy because the skill involved was enormous.

1-0. Carrickmore.

The grass bank sagged. A collective exhalation from a thousand people who had known, intellectually, that this would happen but had allowed themselves, emotionally, to believe it might not. The Carrickmore supporters applauded politely. The commentator said "clinical" twice in one sentence.

Declan did not look at the scoreboard. He looked at his team.

And what he saw, in the thirty seconds after conceding, was the most important data point of the match.

Kev picked the ball from the net. Placed it on the six-yard line. Looked up. Pointed at Sean: "You're fine. Stay there." Pointed at Donal: "Tighter. Tighter on their left." Blue dot.

Shay went to Sean, the young centre-back who had been beaten in the air for the goal. Hand on his head. Two words in his ear. Nobody else could hear them, they were for Sean alone. Sean nodded. Stood taller. Blue dot.

Ciarán, jogging back from the halfway line, clapped twice. Loud. “Same again. Same again. Nothing’s changed.”

Three Blues in the immediate aftermath of conceding.

Declan watched the Carrickmore celebration. Conor jogged away from his teammates with one arm raised, fingers pointing to the sky. The midfielder who’d made the pass stood alone in the centre circle. Nobody came to him. The rest walked back to their positions.

Red dot. Carrickmore.

He turned to Aoife, standing behind him with her own notebook. “We’re fine.”

She looked at the scoreboard. “We’re one-nil down.”

“The scoreboard is the last thing to change.”

Minute twelve. Minute fifteen. Minute eighteen. Carrickmore controlled possession the way a cat controls a room, lazily, full of confidence, with the implication that things could become very energetic if required, but for now this slow, beautiful pressure would suffice.

Ballymore defended, communicated, and waited. With intent. Every clearance directed toward a target rather than hoofed into space. Every goal kick short, to feet, building from the back the way they'd practised. Slowly at first, with the occasional misplaced pass that made the crowd hold its breath, but always with voice. Always with communication.

In the thirteenth minute, Rory chased a lost cause. Ball over the top, clearly the goalkeeper's. He sprinted anyway. Forty metres, arriving just as the keeper collected. It achieved nothing. But three teammates saw him do it, and they ran harder for the next ten minutes.

In the sixteenth minute, Tommo was beaten again by Asare: the same burst of unmatchable pace, the same cross. This time Shay was there. Header clear. He turned to Tommo. "You're doing everything right. He's just quick. Stay with him and I'll cover behind." Tommo nodded. Didn't drop his head. Went again.

Blue. Blue.

In the nineteenth minute, Carrickmore had a free kick thirty metres out. Three players stood over it, arguing about who would take it. Conor wanted it: it was in his range, his angle, his moment. The central midfielder wanted it: he'd been practising this exact scenario. A third player, the left-winger, stood nearby for no discernible reason other than to be in the photograph.

While they argued, the Ballymore wall organised. Shay told each player where to stand. Kev positioned himself. By the time the kick was taken (by Conor, of course, who struck it into the wall), Ballymore had used the thirty seconds of Carrickmore indecision to get every player exactly where they needed to be.

Red dot, Carrickmore. Blue dot, Ballymore.

Twenty minutes.

Declan turned to Aoife. She was already looking at him.

"Reds, us: zero. Blues, us: seven. Reds, them: four. Blues, them: one. Twenty minutes. We've held."

He wrote in the notebook: *R(us): 0. B(us): 7. R(them): 4. B(them): 1. Twenty minutes. Exactly what the model said. They're scoring. But we're playing.*

Aoife was doing her own count.

"Dec."

"What?"

"Their number six. The right-back. He's done it twice now. Receives the ball, passes, and then stops. Completely stops. Like he's done his bit."

"I saw. He doesn't know he's doing it."

"That's the point, isn't it?"

"That's always the point."

Chapter 12: The First Fracture

"It showed up while everything still looked fine."

Minute twenty-two. The ball was at the other end. A Carrickmore throw-in, deep in Ballymore's half. The crowd was watching the thrower, the near-side players jostling for position, the referee ambling into view.

Niamh touched Declan's shoulder.

"Their number six just switched off."

Carrickmore's right-back had received the ball, played it backwards, a safe, functional pass to the centre-half, and then stopped. Not stopped running. Stopped existing as a participant. He stood on the halfway line with his hands on his hips, watching the play develop thirty metres ahead of him. Didn't move into space. Didn't call for a return. Just stood there.

It lasted five seconds. Maybe six. Nobody in the ground noticed, not the crowd, not the commentator, not the Carrickmore bench, not the player himself. He drifted back into the game when the ball was cleared and resumed his position as though nothing had happened.

But Declan had seen it. And Niamh had seen it. And if you'd been watching Aoife's notebook, you'd have seen her pen move too.

Red dot.

"How many is that?" Niamh asked.

"Five. In twenty-two minutes."

"And ours?"

"Zero."

The number sat between them, heavy with implication. Zero Reds in twenty-two minutes against a team that should be taking them apart. It had never happened in Declan's notebook, not in eight weeks of training, not in the handful of matches they'd played since the draw. Zero Reds was not a score but it was a statement.

DECLAN'S MATCH NOTEBOOK – Live

22 minutes

BALLYMORE	**CARRICKMORE**
Reds:	Reds:
(none)	●●●●●
Blues:	Blues:
○○○○○○○	○

#6 – switched off. 5 seconds.
They didn't notice. We did.

Score: 1-0 to them.
Behaviours: 7-1 to us.

The stories don't match.
They don't know it's happening.

Gap closing.

Declan's Match Notebook — 22 minutes

Minute twenty-three. Carrickmore's centre-forward, a tall Latvian named Dāvis who had been signed in January from a Lithuanian club whose name contained four consecutive consonants, received the ball with his back to goal. He had options, a runner left, a runner right, a simple layoff to midfield. He chose to turn. It was a good turn: strong, technically clean, practised ten thousand times in youth academies till it can be done in your sleep but practised with perfect surfaces and no mud and nobody's knee in your lower back.

Shay stood his ground. Didn't dive in. Waited. Dāvis turned into him, and the ball squirted free. Ciarán collected. Played it wide.

Blue dot. Shay. Patience under pressure.

Minute twenty-four. Ballymore worked the ball down the right for the first time in the match: a sequence of short passes that were individually unremarkable but collectively significant. Rory to Ciarán to Tommo, who'd received the ball in space because Carrickmore's left midfielder hadn't tracked back. Tommo looked up. He had a cross on, but the striker was marked. He had a pass back to Ciarán: safe, retain possession. He chose the cross. Not the best decision but he chose it quickly and committed to it, which was better than choosing nothing and getting caught.

The cross was overhit. Sailed over everyone. Goal kick.

But from the sideline, Declan noted: *First time we've been in their half with purpose. Shape held on the transition. Voice held. Good sign.*

Minute twenty-five. Corner to Ballymore. Their first.

The corner had been rehearsed. Not the football of it, though that had been practised too, but the behavioural preparation that preceded it. Declan had told them: *"Your first set piece is a statement. Organise loudly. Make the opposition hear you working together. They're used to teams that go quiet under pressure. Show them a team that gets louder."*

The Ballymore players moved into position with a deliberation that bordered on theatre. Shay pointed. Ciarán called. Rory shouted a code word — "Green!" — that meant absolutely nothing tactically but was designed to create the impression of a team with rehearsed corner routines and coded instructions, which was slightly more organised than the reality, which was "try to get on the end of it."

The corner was taken short. Recycled. Taken again. This time it swung in, a decent delivery from Donal, who had been practising his corner kicks against the community centre wall for three weeks and had twice broken the window of the men's toilet.

The ball found the six-yard box. Bodies everywhere. Ciarán, arriving from deep, from the position he'd been trained to occupy, behind the first cluster, where defenders forget to look, rose above a centre-back who'd lost him because nobody called the runner.

Header. Clean. Firm. Net.

1-1.

The sound from the grass bank was a detonation. A thousand people discovering, all at once, what it felt like to believe. Children screaming. Old men grabbing each other. Dogs barking, whether from excitement or anxiety was unclear and, in the moment, irrelevant.

Ciarán ran to the grass bank, pulling teammates with him. Five, six, seven of them in a pile, arms around each other, faces buried in shoulders. On the sideline, Fr. Tommy blessed himself. Aoife closed her eyes and breathed out.

Declan did not celebrate. He watched the Carrickmore bench.

Graham sat forward, elbows on knees, jaw set. This was what he'd feared: not the goal itself, but what the goal would do to the fragile confidence that was the only thing holding his team together. Devlin, in the stand, was already on his phone.

Red dot. Carrickmore. The chairman responding to an equaliser by disengaging from the match.

"Their chairman is on his phone," Niamh said.

"I know."

"Da, their manager looks like he's going to be sick."

"He can see what's happening. He just can't do anything about it."

Minute twenty-eight. Carrickmore's response to the equaliser was revealing. In a well-functioning team, conceding an unexpected goal produces a collective response: the goalkeeper talks, the defenders reorganise, the midfield tightens, the forwards drop deeper to help. It's not a conscious decision, it's a behavioural reflex born of trust and communication and the shared understanding that when one person is struggling, everyone adjusts.

Carrickmore's response was eleven individual responses happening simultaneously and in contradiction.

Conor demanded the ball be played to him immediately, waving his arm at the centre-back. The centre-back ignored him and played it to the right midfielder. The right midfielder, under no pressure, played a long ball forward that nobody was expecting and nobody was in position to receive. Dāvis, the centre-forward, sprinted for it anyway as did the left winger, and they arrived in the same space at the same time, competing with each other rather than the opposition.

From the stand, Roberta typed a note on her phone: *Post-equaliser response: no collective reorganisation. Individual frustration responses. Time to restore structure: still pending. Compare to their behaviour after scoring: also no collective response. Pattern: this team doesn't have a shared behavioural vocabulary.*

Minute thirty-two. Ballymore were growing. Carrickmore still had the ball more than them, but the confidence was shifting, the voice was rising, and the thousand small signals that Declan tracked were all pointing the same way.

Rory won a header in midfield. It was a genuine fifty-fifty contest where superior physicality should decide, and Rory was neither taller nor stronger than his opponent. But he wanted it more, and wanting-it-more is not a cliché in behavioural terms; it's a measurable thing: arriving a fraction earlier, jumping a fraction higher, committing a fraction more completely to the challenge. Rory won the header. Played it to Ciarán. Transition.

Nothing came of it but that didn't matter. The intent was the data.

Minute thirty-five. The moment Declan would later describe as the most important Blue of the half.

Shay threw his body across a Conor Fitzpatrick shot from twelve metres. It was brave, the ball was struck hard and from close range, and Shay couldn't have known, as he launched himself sideways, whether it would hit his face or his chest or his arms or find its way past him into the net. But he went anyway. Block. Corner.

The ball cannoned off his ribcage and he lay on the ground for a moment, eyes closed, processing pain. Then he got up. Turned to Sean, the young centre-back beside him.

"My fault," he said. Held up a hand.

It wasn't his fault. The shot had come from a turnover in midfield, nowhere near Shay's area of responsibility. The young centre-back had been the one who'd lost possession. Everyone in the ground knew it. Sean knew it.

But afterwards Sean stood taller. And for the rest of the half, he won every header.

Blue dot.

Minute thirty-eight. Carrickmore scored.

It was a good goal. A reminder of why they were three divisions above Ballymore and why thirty-six percent was thirty-six percent and not ninety-six. A quick break from a Ballymore corner, the left-back intercepted, played it forward with one touch, the midfielder drove forty metres upfield while Ballymore were still reorganising from the set piece, slipped it wide to Asare, whose cross found Dāvis at the far post. Clinical finish. Head. Corner of the net.

2-1. Carrickmore.

Seven minutes to halftime. The grass bank went quiet again, not the stunned silence of the first goal, but the resigned silence of people recalibrating their expectations. The commentary on local radio used the word "inevitable." A man on the grass bank packed up his fold-out chair.

But within ten seconds of the ball hitting the net — Declan counted them, his hand on his watch, because this was measurable and measurements mattered — Ballymore had reset.

Kev placed the ball. Organised the defence with two pointed instructions. Shay positioned himself and said four words to Sean: "Same thing. Stay with me." Ciarán, jogging back from the Carrickmore half, clapped twice, the same clap, the same rhythm, the same words as after the first goal: "Same again. Nothing's changed."

Nobody's head dropped. Nobody looked at the bench. Nobody's shoulders went.

They looked at each other.

Declan's pen: *Blue. Blue. Blue. Response identical to the first goal. The pattern holds. Resilience confirmed. They've been trained and it's taken.*

On the Carrickmore bench, Graham watched the Ballymore response with the nauseated recognition of a man who could see exactly what was happening and could do nothing about it. He'd been a coach long enough to know that a team that responds to setbacks with collective composure is more dangerous than a team that responds to success with individual celebration. He also knew that the opposite was true of his own team, and that the man responsible for that was sitting in the stand checking the share price of Larkfield Holdings on his phone.

Halftime whistle. Carrickmore 2, Ballymore 1.

Pearse O'Sullivan informed his listeners that "the home side have given a tremendous account of themselves and will feel hard done by to go in behind." He was right, though not for the reasons he thought. The scoreboard said Carrickmore were comfortable. Declan's notebook said they were on the edge of a cliff and about to blunder off it.

Chapter 13: A Tale of Two Dressing Rooms

“Fifteen individuals will struggle to beat a team.”

THE HOME DRESSING ROOM

The corridor between the two dressing rooms was eight metres long, with a concrete floor that had been painted blue at some point in the previous century and a strip light that hummed at a frequency specifically designed to make people anxious. One door led left, one door led right, and the eight metres between them contained, at that moment, the distance between two entirely different philosophies of leadership.

Declan closed the door.

The room was small and warm and smelled of mud and Deep Heat and that musk of fifteen men who had just spent forty-five minutes doing something they would remember for the rest of their lives. Players sat on benches, on the floor, on the edge of the physio table that Niamh had commandeered for water bottles. Shay was in the corner, applying an ice pack to his ribs with the stoicism of a man who regarded pain as an administrative inconvenience. Rory sat with his head between his knees, breathing hard, legs trembling with lactic acid and adrenaline.

Niamh moved through the room with water and half-time oranges. She didn't speak to the players. She'd been briefed by her father on the protocol. Halftime was behavioural territory. Her job was logistics. But she was watching, and she was learning, and later she would tell Declan what she'd seen: that every player in the room was making eye contact with at least one other player. That nobody was isolated. That the body language said *disappointed but not defeated* and the difference between those two states was the distance between a team that comes out fighting and a team that comes out folding.

Declan waited for the room to settle. Thirty seconds. He'd learned long ago that the first voice in a halftime dressing room sets the temperature for the next forty-five minutes.

"I want to tell you what I saw," he said. "Not the score."

He opened the notebook.

"Zero Reds."

He let it sit.

"From us. Zero. Not one moment where someone disengaged, blamed a teammate, lost composure, or stopped communicating. In forty-five minutes against a team from three divisions above us. Zero."

Faces looked up. Rory's head came up from between his knees.

"In eight weeks, I've never recorded zero. Years of watching matches from all codes, I've never recorded zero."

He turned a page.

"Twelve Blues. Unprompted communication. Covering for each other. Organising after conceding."

He looked at specific players.

"Shay. You took the blame for Sean's mistake. Sean played free for the rest of the half because of that."

Shay nodded, once. Said nothing.

"Rory. Provoked twice. Zero retaliations. That's the hardest thing in sport and you're doing it."

Rory's fingers moved unbidden to the tape on his wrist.

"Kev: three goal kicks, all short, all to feet, all while a thousand people behind you wanted you to hoof it. That takes more courage than you think."

Then Declan switched.

"Now. Their behaviours."

"Six Reds from them. Number six switched off twice. Number nine was refused the ball by his own midfielder. Centre-backs argued after our goal. Their chairman was on his phone when we scored."

He paused.

“Their chairman. Was on his phone. When his team conceded a goal in the FAI Cup.”

Niamh spoke from the corner. She’d been standing so quietly that several players had forgotten she was there.

“Their number nine hasn’t spoken to a teammate since the thirty-fifth minute. Not a word. Ten minutes of silence from a centre-forward.”

Declan nodded. His daughter was seeing what he saw.

“We’re one goal down and we’re winning this match.”

He held their eyes.

“The scoreboard just doesn’t know it yet.”

Silence.

Ciarán spoke. “I played under this man when I was sixteen and he couldn’t kick a ball to save his life.”

Laughter.

“Told us the same thing before a county semi though: don’t watch the scoreboard, watch each other. We won by three points. Trust him.”

Shay stood. The room went quiet the way rooms went quiet when Shay stood.

"Forty-five minutes. One goal. Leave everything you have on that pitch. Doesn't matter what happens after. This is ours."

Declan: "Second half. One priority. *Score the next goal.* That's all. Find the next goal and we'll worry about the one after that when it comes. Focus."

He held up one finger.

"One thing. One priority. One half."

They stood. Shay led them out. Last to sit down, first to stand up. Temperature set.

THE AWAY DRESSING ROOM

Eight metres away, through a concrete corridor with a humming strip light, the temperature was different.

Devlin had come down from the stand. His shoes, Italian leather, inappropriate for the occasion, overcoat and mood had all been ruined by a muddy field in Ballymore. He stood in the centre of a dressing room that was marginally smaller than the home one and significantly more crowded, because it contained not just fifteen players and a coaching staff but also a chairman, two board members, and the gravitational distortion that occurs when a man who is used to being the most important person in every room enters a room where he is the least qualified person to speak.

Graham sat on the bench. He had notes. He had a plan for the second half: a tactical adjustment that involved dropping the defensive line deeper, pushing Conor into a more central position where his tendency to shoot would at least be from better angles, and switching to a three-man midfield to combat Ciarán's influence. It was a good plan. He'd been thinking about it since the twenty-fifth minute.

Devlin looked around the room. The players expected anger. They'd seen his face on the walk down from the stand: jaw set, phone pocketed for once, moving with the controlled urgency of a man who was used to fixing things that had gone wrong.

"Right," he said. "I owe some people in this room an apology."

The room went still. This was not in anyone's script.

"Graham told me two weeks ago to prepare properly for this match. Said this Ballymore team were better than they had any right to be. I said relax." He looked at Graham. "You were right. I should have listened."

Graham said nothing. His face gave away nothing.

"Roberta told me three weeks ago that our communication was breaking down. She showed me the data. I said file it." He looked toward the back of the room, where Roberta stood behind the board members, and nodded once. "You were right too."

Roberta's expression didn't change, but she straightened slightly.

"What's done is done." Devlin's voice shifted. This was the voice that had built Larkfield Holdings from a two-man consultancy into a company that employed four hundred people. The voice that had convinced banks to lend, investors to invest, and a football club to believe it could compete with anyone. It was a good voice. Confident without being loud. Direct without being aggressive. The voice of a man who genuinely believed what he was saying.

"But here's what hasn't changed: you are the best players in this division. That's not opinion, that's fact. Every one of you is here because you earned the right to be here. You've trained five days a week on the best facilities in the country. You've got skills, fitness, experience that no Junior team can match. That's your edge and nothing that's happened out there in forty-five minutes changes it."

He pointed toward the pitch.

"They're playing well. Credit to them, they're well organised and they're fighting for everything. But this still comes down to quality. To capability. And there, you have them beat. Every one of you is better than the man opposite you. So go out there and show them what that means. You’re still winning! Not by as much as you should be and it’s time to drive that advantage home. Play harder. Play faster. Use the ability that got you here. "

It was, by any standard, a good speech. Devlin could read a room. He could admit fault. He could rally people. These were not small skills, and they were the reasons he'd built what he'd built.

The problem wasn’t that it was wrong, it was factually correct, but it was still drawing the same, wrong conclusion.

The room responded the way talented individuals respond to inspirational speeches from authority figures: they nodded, felt briefly motivated, and absorbed nothing that would change what they actually did on the pitch.

Conor was looking at his phone. Openly, with the relaxed confidence of a man who had scored and therefore considered his contribution discharged. Nobody told him to put it away. Nobody would.

Graham opened his notepad. He'd been planning to suggest dropping the defensive line deeper, pushing Conor central, switching to a three-man midfield. He looked at Devlin, who was already turning to the door.

"Graham, anything to add?"

He wanted to say: Talk to each other. Cover for each other. Put your damn phones down and be a team, for the love of God, be a team, because the fifteen individuals you're choosing to be are about to be beaten by fifteen men who earn less in a year than you spend on headbands.

He said: "What Mark said. Give it everything."

In the corner, the defenders were still arguing about the set piece that had led to Ballymore's equaliser, a disagreement about marking responsibility that had roots in a training-ground incident weeks ago and that Graham had been told, by Devlin, to "let sort itself out because senior players manage themselves." It had not sorted itself out. It had calcified into a grudge that was now live on the biggest stage of their season, unresolved, toxic, and about to cost them.

Dāvis, the centre-forward, sat alone. He had scored. Nobody had mentioned it.

Roberta stood at the back of the room, behind the board members. She typed a note on her phone:

Halftime. He admitted he was wrong. First time I've seen that. Good speech — genuine, humble, rallying. And completely beside the point. He diagnosed capability when the problem is behaviour. Like prescribing vitamins for a broken leg. The other dressing room is eight metres and a world away. I'd give anything to know what's happening in it.

HALFTIME — Two Rooms, Two Worlds

BALLYMORE

Reds: 0

Blues:

○○○○○○○○○○○○ (12)

Coach speaks first.

Data shared.

Players make eye contact.

"We're winning this match. The scoreboard just doesn't know it yet."

Model conditions:

✓ Blues > 4

✓ Their Reds > 3

✓ Our Reds = 0

→ **54%**

CARRICKMORE

Reds:

●●●●●● (6)

Blues:

○ (1)

Chairman speaks first.

Blame assigned.

Star on phone.

Two defenders arguing.

"More intensity. Win your battles."

The emptiest instruction in sport.

Mgt bhvr: 0.3

× Coach: 0.4

× Team: 0.5

× Capability: 9

= **Eff. perf: 0.54**

Halftime: Two Rooms, Two Worlds

Chapter 14: Fifty-Four Percent

"The dam is breaking and they can't stop it."

Second half. The teams emerged to a noise that had changed character during the interval. The Ballymore crowd had been quiet going into halftime, processing the deficit, but something had happened in the fifteen minutes of tea and oranges and toilet queues. The mood had shifted. It wasn't optimism exactly, these were people who had lived in a small town long enough to be genetically resistant to optimism, but it was something adjacent. Curiosity. The realisation that whatever they were watching, it wasn't the mismatch they'd expected.

The first five minutes would test that curiosity immediately.

Carrickmore came out hard. Hard in the Devlin sense: emotional urgency, bodies forward, no structure. The "play harder" instruction had been absorbed by the players as emotional urgency rather than tactical intelligence, and it looked like what Declan would later describe in his notebook as "eleven fires in eleven locations, no fire service."

Three players pressed the ball-carrier at once. The other eight watched.

"Look," Declan said to Aoife. "Three on the ball. Eight standing. They're panicking."

In the first four minutes of the second half, Carrickmore committed seven players forward on two separate occasions, leaving gaps behind them that Ballymore weren't yet brave enough to exploit but that Declan could see from the sideline like open wounds.

Minute forty-nine. Conor demanded a pass from the centre-back. Received it with his back to goal. Had a simple layoff to the midfielder, safe, retain possession, recycle. Had an overlap on the right, a forward pass that would put Asare in behind, seventy percent chance of creating a crossing opportunity.

Conor turned. Tried to beat two defenders. Lost the ball. Didn't track back. Jogged — jogged — while Ballymore transitioned and Ciarán drove forward and the crowd leaned forward as one.

Red dot. Carrickmore. The individual over the team, again.

"That's seven," Declan said.

"Seven Reds?"

"Since the match started. And they're accelerating."

Minute fifty-one. Two Carrickmore midfielders both went for the same ball, neither calling, neither looking, both assuming the other would leave it. Collision, shoulder to shoulder, and the ball squirted free to Ciarán, who fed it wide.

Red dot. Communication breakdown. Minute fifty-one.

Minute fifty-two. Conor, through on the right, had a simple square ball to the centre-forward. Dāvis was unmarked, eight metres from goal, arm raised, calling loudly enough that the crowd could hear him. It was, by any rational measure, a certain goal. The ninety-percent option.

Conor shot instead. From a tight angle. From the exact angle Kev had been shown video of. Blocked. The ball deflected wide. Corner.

Dāvis threw his arms up. Turned away. Said something in Latvian that didn't require translation. For the rest of the match, he would not make another run into the box.

Red dot. Red dot.

"Dec," Aoife said. "Nine Reds. The model says—"

"I know what the model says."

"Nine Reds puts the probability at—"

"Aoife. I know."

The probability of Ballymore winning, adjusted for live behavioural data, had ticked past fifty percent for the first time in the match. The scoreboard said 2-1 to Carrickmore. The notebook said something else entirely.

Minute fifty-five. Paddy Rourke played a long ball forward: hopeful, aimless, the football equivalent of throwing a rock into the dark and hoping it hit something. It was intercepted by Sean, who had spent the second half growing in confidence with every minute, feeding off Shay's calm, playing passes he wouldn't have attempted in the first half.

Ballymore transitioned. Three passes. Simple. Short. Passes that don't make highlight reels, that local radio ignores, that never appear in analytics dashboards. Passes that win football matches.

Ciarán to Rory. Rory to Donal, overlapping on the left. Donal to Ciarán, who'd continued his run because someone had called, someone had listened, and someone had moved.

Seventy percent. Seventy percent. Seventy percent.

Ciarán was thirty metres from goal with three options. He took a fraction of a second to assess, long enough to see, short enough that the window didn't close. Played it through the centre, on the ground, into the space between the centre-backs, where Damo was arriving at a flat sprint from deep. Nobody had tracked him. Carrickmore's defenders had stopped communicating fourteen minutes ago.

Damo reached the ball. Controlled it. Not cleanly, with the inside of his right foot and a stumble. He looked up. The goalkeeper came out. Damo didn't think, didn't calculate percentages. Damo hit it. Low, hard and across the keeper. Inside the far post. Not clean. Off his shin, off a divot, across the line.

The net rippled.

2-2.

The sound was different from the first equaliser. That had been a detonation: surprise, joy, release. This was deeper. This was a thousand people realising, with a conviction that settled in their chests, that what they were witnessing was not a fluke. The first goal could have been luck. The second was a pattern.

Damo ran to the grass bank with his arms spread wide and a face that suggested he wasn't entirely sure this was real. He was engulfed by teammates. From somewhere in the pile, Ciarán's voice: "Again. Again. We go again."

On the sideline, Declan turned to Aoife.

"They're in freefall. Watch the Reds now."

"Dec—"

"The equaliser will accelerate it. Watch. Within five minutes, their discipline will collapse. The substitutions will come. They'll be the wrong substitutions, made for the wrong reasons, by the wrong person."

Aoife looked at him.

"How do you know that?"

"Because the First Red was never on the pitch. And the man responsible for the First Red is sitting in the stand, and he's about to do what he always does when the dashboard turns red: throw resources at the problem without understanding what the problem is."

In the stand, Devlin put his phone in his pocket for the first time all match. He was paying attention now. But attention without understanding just leads to louder interference.

Minute fifty-eight. Carrickmore kicked off. Played it backwards. The ball went from the centre-forward to the midfielder to the centre-back in three passes that contained no forward movement and no purpose beyond the desire to have the ball somewhere safe while the emotional turbulence of conceding settled into something manageable. It was the footballing equivalent of holding your breath.

Ballymore pressed. Coordinated. Patient. Rory pushed up. Ciarán closed the passing lane. Donal pressed the full-back. The ball went backwards again. And again. Carrickmore were recycling possession without purpose, trapped in their own half by a team that had been taught to press as a unit rather than as a collection of individuals.

Minute fifty-nine. Paddy Rourke, under pressure from Rory's closing run, played a pass to his centre-back partner that was underhit and slightly behind the receiver. The centre-back adjusted, controlled, looked up and found himself face-to-face with Ciarán, who had anticipated the pass, read the body language, and arrived a half-second before the ball.

Ciarán didn't tackle. He didn't need to. The centre-back, startled, turned back and played the ball to his goalkeeper. The goalkeeper, with no obvious option, hoofed it long. It went exactly to Shay, who headed it down to Rory, who laid it off, and Ballymore had possession again in the Carrickmore half.

Nothing came of it. The move broke down two passes later. But Carrickmore's defenders were no longer passing with confidence. They were passing with fear.

Red dot. Red dot. The Reds were no longer individual incidents; they were a systemic collapse. Each one caused the next.

Minute sixty-two. Ballymore had a throw-in deep in the Carrickmore half. Ciarán threw it long, a flat throw that carried twenty-five metres and landed in the box. Scramble. The ball bounced off three players, hit the post, and was cleared. The crowd gasped, then roared.

Minute sixty-three. Rory won possession in midfield. Played it forward to Damo. Damo controlled, turned, saw Ciarán overlapping. Played it. Ciarán's cross was too high, over the bar, everyone.

But the pattern was clear to anyone watching the behaviours rather than the scoreboard. Ballymore were creating chances through collective movement: passes, runs, overlaps, communication. Carrickmore were defending through individual effort: last-ditch tackles, goalkeeper saves, balls cleared to nobody.

The capability gap was still there. If anything, more visible. But Carrickmore's individual skill was isolated from any collective structure now, and isolated skill has a ceiling.

Declan to Aoife: "This is what it looks like when the multiplier hits zero. The capability is still nine. But nine times zero is zero."

"It's not quite zero."

"Close enough. Close enough for us."

Chapter 15: Three Breaths

"Same player. Different behaviour. Different outcome."

Minute sixty-five.

Rory's legs were burning. Not the manageable burn of an early-season training session, the deep, acidic burn that arrives in the last third of a match when the body's glycogen is gone and the muscles are running on willpower and whatever remained of the half-time oranges. His hamstrings felt like they'd been replaced with warm elastic bands. His calves were cramping at the edges. Every sprint now was a negotiation between what his mind wanted and what his body could deliver, and the terms were getting worse.

The Carrickmore centre-back was still accelerating. Seventy kilometres a week on proper pitches, nutritionist-managed diet. The physical gap between them was widening with every minute.

A long ball. High, hanging, dropping into the space between the halfway line and the edge of the box.

Both went for it. They arrived together but the centre-back arrived first. Half a stride.

The ball was headed clear. Rory went to ground, not from the aerial challenge but from the shoulder that followed it, late enough to be cynical but early enough to be deniable. He lay on the Ballymore turf, face down, tasting grass and copper.

The centre-back stood over him.

And then, low enough that only Rory could hear, the centre-back spoke.

"Stay down, kid. This isn't your level."

Two selves. The one that wants to react, immediate, violent. And the one that can see the whole pitch. The consequences branching forward: *react, get sent off, let the team down, be the old Rory.*

For most of Rory Kavanagh's life, the reactive self had won.

At sixteen, it had won when a youth coach at a League of Ireland academy had told him he "lacked discipline" and Rory had told the coach what he could do with his discipline using vocabulary that was creative, anatomically improbable, and career-ending. Released the next morning.

At eighteen, it had won when a Sunday League defender stood on his ankle deliberately and Rory responded with an elbow that earned a straight red and a six-match ban and the quiet, devastating verdict of his father: *You could have been something, Rory.*

At twenty-one, it had won in a pub car park on a Tuesday night, and the only thing that had saved him from a conviction was the other man's decision not to press charges and Rory's mother's tears in the solicitor's office.

Declan had shown him the data. In his kitchen, over tea, with the notebook open and the numbers plain.

"How many times have you lost your head, Rory?"

"I don't know. A few."

"Twelve. In the last three years, twelve incidents where you reacted instead of responded. Red cards, fights, walk-offs. Twelve. And what happened after each one?"

Rory had known the answer. It was the answer he lived with.

"We lost."

"Eleven out of twelve. Ninety-two percent. Your reaction didn't just cost you, it cost everyone who depended on you."

And then the question that had changed everything, though Rory hadn't known it at the time:

"What if the next time it happens — and it will happen, because it always happens — what if you could buy yourself three seconds? Just three seconds be-

tween the stimulus and the response. What would you do with those three seconds?"

"I don't know."

"You'd see the pitch."

He lay on the grass. The centre-back's words, *Stay down, kid. This isn't your level*, hung in the air, burning.

His right hand clenched. Jaw tight. The reactive self was screaming. He could feel it in his chest, that white, electric rush of rage that narrowed the world to a single point: the man standing over him, the injustice, the disrespect. His vision was tunnelling.

The tape. Left wrist.

He didn't look at it. He felt it, the slight pressure of the zinc oxide against his skin, the physical anchor that connected his body to a practice he'd been training for eight weeks, every session, every time Declan had made him stand on the edge of the training pitch and close his eyes and breathe while a teammate shouted at him, stood over him, said things designed to trigger exactly this response.

"The tape is the trigger," Declan had said. *"Not for the anger. For the breathing. Touch the tape, you breathe. It's a circuit. Build it until it's automatic."*

Breath one.

The anger was white-hot, present and enormous. He could feel his heartbeat in his ears. The breath didn't remove the anger but sat alongside it, a calm second voice in a room where someone is screaming.

Breath two.

Still there. The anger was still there, and the centre-back was still standing over him, and the crowd was still watching, and the referee was ambling over with the unhurried pace of a man who had seen this kind of thing a thousand times and was already reaching for his pocket. But Rory could see around it. And that was the difference, the entire difference, the thing that the tape and the breathing and the eight weeks of practice had built. The anger was still in the centre of his vision but it was no longer the whole frame. Around the edges, blurred but present, he could see the pitch. His teammates. The ball, rolling free toward the right side of the field.

Breath three.

He saw the pitch.

He got up. Slowly. Without drama, without the theatrical stagger of a man milking a foul, without the aggressive spring of a man about to start a fight. He stood up the way a person stands up when they've decided something, and what he'd decided was more important than anything that had happened in the previous five seconds.

He didn't look at the defender. Didn't speak. Didn't gesture. Looked for the ball.

The referee awarded the free kick. Rory walked away from the centre-back with the deliberate calm of a man who was spending every remaining unit of self-control on the act of walking and could not afford to allocate any of it to expression.

On the sideline, Declan's pen stopped moving. He'd been frozen since Rory went to ground, not breathing, not blinking, waiting to see which Rory got up. The old Rory or the new Rory. The reactive Rory or the choosing Rory.

He saw the choosing Rory pull himself up from the ground.

Declan exhaled. Wrote in the notebook: *R.K. Down. Provoked. Three breaths. Got up clean. Blue.*

Aoife, beside him: "Was that—?"

"That was everything. That was the whole programme in fifteen seconds."

Free kick. Ballymore. Thirty metres out, left of centre.

Ciarán took it quickly. Short, to Shay, who'd come forward for the set piece. Shay controlled it, looked up, played a long ball into the channel behind the Carrickmore right-back, the one who'd been switching off.

The ball was perfect. Weighted, angled, dropping into the space between the full-back and the centre-back, exactly where a runner would arrive if a runner was making the run.

Rory was making the run.

He shouldn't have been able to. His legs were gone. The lactic acid had been building since the fiftieth minute, and the challenge that put him on the ground had added a throbbing pain in his left hip that would, over the next three days, turn into a bruise the size and colour of an aubergine. His body was near finished but his mind was not.

He ran. Thirty metres. The centre-back, caught flat-footed by the quick free kick, turned and pursued. For ten metres, they were level. For twenty metres, the centre-back was closing. At thirty metres, Rory reached the ball a half-step ahead because the centre-back had assumed it was a footrace and footraces are won by the faster runner, but this was not a footrace, it was a test of anticipation, and Rory had started running before the ball was played because he'd seen Shay's body shape, seen the space, and committed to the run on faith.

He reached the ball. Controlled it with the inside of his right foot, a touch that was, by any technical standard, ugly. The ball bounced off his shin, bobbled, and sat up awkwardly two metres in front of him. But he was through. One-on-one with the space, the goalkeeper coming out, the goal open.

He looked up.

He had two options.

Shoot. Twenty metres out. The goalkeeper was off his line but not committed. A well-struck shot — and Rory could strike a ball, this was never in doubt — had maybe a thirty-percent chance. Not bad odds. Old Rory shoots. Every time. Without looking. Without thinking. Because shooting was what Rory Kavanagh did, and the highlight reel was the only metric that mattered when you were trying to prove that a youth coach and a Sunday League ban and a pub car park were not the story of your life.

Or.

Damo. Arriving at the back post, arms up, unmarked because nobody had tracked his run, because tracking runners from deep requires communication, and Carrickmore had stopped communicating forty minutes ago. Damo was six metres from an open goal. The pass to him was a fifteen-metre ball along the ground, weighted, to his feet. Seventy percent. Maybe higher.

The tape on his wrist.

Old Rory shoots.

New Rory saw the pitch and played the pass.

It was perfect. Low. Weighted. Arriving clear at Damo's feet, one touch, rough, imperfect ... and in. Low. Left corner. The goalkeeper had no chance because the goalkeeper was still in no man's land, caught between the shot he expected and the pass he didn't.

3-2. Ballymore led.

The sound.

There are noises that human beings produce collectively that transcend the sum of their individual voices. A thousand people, on a grass bank behind a goal, watching a plasterer from Cahir score a goal that puts their village team ahead of a professional side in the FAI Cup, produce a sound that is felt in the chest before it reaches the ears.

The grass bank emptied. People poured down the slope toward the pitch, stopped only by a rope line that had been put there by Paddy Joe more in hope than expectation. Children were screaming. Dogs were barking. An elderly man in a flat cap was crying and didn't care who saw. Pearse O'Sullivan, on local radio, was producing sounds that were technically English but had been processed through such intense emotion that they were closer to speaking in tongues.

Damo ran. Away from the goal, toward the grass bank, toward his teammates who were already converging on him like iron filings to a magnet. He was caught first by Ciarán, then by Rory, then by all of them, a pile of bodies and joy and disbelief and the ecstasy of people who had done something together that none of them could have done alone.

On the sideline, Declan stood motionless. Notebook in one hand. Pen in the other. The match wasn't over. The notebook wasn't finished.

Aoife grabbed his arm. "Dec."

"I know."

"Dec, we're winning."

"I know. But it's not over yet."

He looked at the notebook. He looked at the clock. He looked at his team, disentangling themselves from the celebration, Shay already pulling players upright, Ciarán already clapping: "Not yet. Not yet. There's twenty-five minutes."

And he looked across the pitch at the Carrickmore bench, where Graham Welsh sat with his head in his hands, and at the stand, where Mark Devlin was standing, phone in hand, with the expression of a man who was about to make everything worse.

Rory was on his knees. The sprint, the pass, the emotion. His legs had simply stopped. He was on his knees on the Ballymore turf, and for a moment the sound of the crowd was very far away and the sky was very close and he was a twenty-three-year-old from a housing estate in Cahir who had just chosen the team over himself for the first time in his life.

Shay found him. Hand on the back of his neck. The grip was firm, warm, grounding.

"Not yet. Twenty-five minutes. Focus."

Rory touched the tape. Nodded.

Shay pulled him up.

From the notebook: *R.K. — fouled, provoked, three breaths. Got up clean. Won the free. Made the run. Saw the pass. Played the pass. Blue. Blue. Blue. Same player. Different behaviour. Different outcome. This is what it looks like.*

Chapter 16: The Final Fifteen

"The capability gap was real but the behaviour gap was bigger."

Minute sixty-nine. Devlin made his move.

He'd been on the phone since the Ballymore goal. Not calling anyone in particular. Just cycling through contacts with the restless energy of a man who needed to be doing something just to be doing something but had nothing useful to do.

The walkie-talkie crackled. Graham heard Devlin's voice, tinny and distorted by the cheap radio but perfectly clear in its intent.

"Make changes. Fresh legs. Three substitutions."

Graham closed his eyes. Opened them.

"Mark, better make one targeted change. I want to bring Kelly on for Doyle, freshen up the right side, keep the structure—"

"Three changes, Graham. Three. We need energy."

"Energy isn't the problem. The problem is—"

"Three. Changes."

Silence.

Graham sighed and turned to his bench. He had four substitutes. The fourth was Kelly, a twenty-year-old with pace and no positional sense, signed in January on the basis of a twenty-second video clip shown to Devlin at a golf tournament.

He had thirty seconds to prepare three substitutes who needed fifteen minutes.

“Kelly, Ward, Brennan. You’re on.”

Kelly looked up from the bench with the startled expression of a man who had been told, based on the scoreline and his recent experience, that he would not be needed today.

“For who?”

“Asare, Murray, and Devitt.”

“What do I—”

“Just get on.”

The three substitutes entered the field with energy and confusion, not sure what to do but fully aware they needed to be doing something, pressing forward, demanding the ball, making runs into spaces that had been carefully left empty for tactical reasons they hadn’t been briefed on and couldn’t be expected to understand. It was like pouring petrol on a campfire: dramatic, bright, and ultimately destructive.

Declan turned to Aoife. “He’s just made it worse.”

“Who made the substitution?”

Declan looked at the stand. “Not the coach.”

“The chairman?”

“From the stand. Watch: within ten minutes, whatever structure they had left will dissolve.”

It took six.

Minute seventy-two. Ward, the central midfielder substitute, was supposed to sit in front of the defence. Graham had told him this in the thirty seconds available. Ward pushed forward. Nobody filled in behind him. Ciarán drifted into the gap, received the ball, turned, and played a pass that split the Carrickmore defence. Another runner from deep, arriving unmarked. Same gap. Same silence where communication should have been.

This time, Damo’s shot was saved. The goalkeeper, the one Carrickmore player who had performed with consistent competence all match, pushed it wide. Corner.

The crowd groaned. Then roared. The pattern was visible now even to people who knew nothing about football. Because Ballymore had momentum.

Minute seventy-five. Carrickmore equalised.

A scrappy goal from a disintegrating match: a corner, poorly cleared by a Ballymore defender whose legs had gone, a scramble in the six-yard box, the ball bouncing off three players and a post before a Carrickmore substitute, Brennan, hooked it in from two metres with his shin.

3-3.

Carrickmore still had the capability advantage and that meant they were still dangerous. Even as the dam broke.

The grass bank went quiet. The quiet of people who'd been carried to the edge of something extraordinary and felt it being taken back.

In the stand, Devlin sat down. In his framework, the equaliser justified the substitutions. He didn't notice that the goal had come from chaos rather than design, and that the chaos was the thing his substitutions had created.

On the sideline, Declan watched his team.

The goal didn't matter but what happened next would.

Kev picked the ball from the net. Placed it. Looked up. Began organising the defence with pointed instructions: the same instructions, the same voice, the same calm. Shay stood behind the back line:

"Nothing's changed. Stay together." Ciarán, in midfield, clapped twice: "Next goal. Next goal."

Rory, running on nothing, but defiance and willpower and a strip of zinc oxide tape on his left wrist. He touched the tape, found another ounce of reserve and ran.

Blue. Blue. Blue. Blue.

The response was identical to the response at 1-0. Identical to 2-1. The same collective reorganisation, the same verbal cues, the same composure. No blame. No panic. No looking at the bench. No heads dropping. No shoulders going.

They looked at each other.

Declan exhaled. He'd been holding his breath and hadn't known it.

"They're still there," he said.

Aoife looked at him. Her eyes were shining and her notebook was forgotten in her hand.

"The equaliser didn't break the behaviours." He added. "We're still in this."

Minute eighty. A lull. The match had the exhausted, ragged quality that cup ties develop in the final ten minutes, neither team with the energy or structure to sustain an attack, both teams making mistakes that would have been punished earlier but were now absorbed by the equal and opposite mistakes of the opposition.

Minute eighty-two. The red card.

Kelly, the substitute, had been on the pitch for twelve minutes. In that time, he had received no tactical instruction from the bench, no positional guidance from his teammates, and no briefing on the opposition. He was operating blind, a quick, talented, twenty-year-old player who had been placed in a high-stakes environment with no preparation, no support, and no framework for decision-making.

Donal received the ball on the touchline and turned inside. Kelly was the nearest defender. He should have stayed on his feet, shown Donal down the line, waited for cover.

Kelly lunged. Late. Studs showing. A challenge born of frustration and confusion.

The referee didn't hesitate. Straight red. The card was out before Kelly had finished sliding.

Kelly sat on the grass, stunned. He looked at the bench. Graham's face told him everything he needed to know. Behind Graham, in the stand, Devlin was already leaving his seat.

Carrickmore down to ten men. Eight minutes of match time remaining, plus whatever the referee added on.

The red card might have been Kelly's but the First Red was Devlin's.

Minute eighty-four.

The match had shifted. Ten men against eleven, but Carrickmore still had the better individuals, and individuals matter when the game becomes open and desperate. Conor Fitzpatrick received the ball thirty metres from goal. The crowd held its breath, both sets of supporters, for different reasons.

Conor had two options.

The first: the overlapping full-back, unmarked on the right side. The full-back was waving. Shouting. A simple pass and a cross would put the ball into a box where Carrickmore's height advantage would matter. Seventy percent.

The second: go alone.

Conor didn't register the full-back.

It wasn't that the full-back was invisible. He was five metres away, in clear space, waving his arm and shouting with the increasingly frantic energy of a man who knows he's being ignored and can't understand why. The full-back was as visible as it was possible for a human being in a fluorescent kit to be.

Conor didn't see him because Conor's incentive structure had trained his eyes to see one thing: the goal. Bonuses for goals scored, nothing for assists. And the system got what it optimised for. Conor went alone.

He beat the first defender with a drop of the shoulder that was, again, genuinely brilliant, scouts would have salivated, coaches would have despaired. Individual excellence in a team sport. A pianist performing a concerto solo while the orchestra sits in silence.

Then he met Shay. And Shay, thirty-five years old, aching, exhausted, with ice-pack welts on his ribs and grass stains on his knees, stood his ground. Didn't dive in. Didn't commit. Waited with the patience of a man who had been doing this since Conor was in primary school and who understood, in his bones, that attackers who go alone eventually run out of space and that defenders who stand still eventually get the ball.

Conor tried to go around him. Left. The ball ran slightly ahead of him, fatigue, or the pitch, or the accumulated weight of eighty-four minutes. It was a centimetre too far. Shay's foot was there. The ball rolled free.

Ciarán picked it up. Looked up. Played it wide to Rory.

Three passes. Simple. Short. Seventy percent. Seventy percent. Seventy percent.

Rory, exhausted, empty, running on whatever was left after eighty-four minutes and a transformation that had cost him more energy than any match he'd ever played, received the ball on the right. He had a shot on. From here, fifteen metres, the goalkeeper slightly off his line, maybe thirty percent. The old percentage.

He didn't shoot.

He looked up. Saw Donal on the right, overlapping. Played it. Donal crossed — first time, low, hard, into the corridor.

Damo, arriving at the back post again. Unmarked. Again.

And Damo struck the ball with the honest, full-bodied commitment of a man who played football because he loved it. The ball hit the net before the goalkeeper moved.

4-3.

The sound that came from the grass bank was something none of them had heard before and none of them would forget. A community discovering that the story they'd been told about themselves — too small, too poor, too left behind — was wrong.

The grass bank didn't empty this time. It levitated. A thousand people rising together, held together by a sound they were making and couldn't control, a sound that boomed across Ballymore and that would be described, later, in the pub, as "something else entirely".

Damo was on the ground, five teammates on top of him, the noise, the meaning, the sheer physical impossibility of remaining vertical. He was under there somewhere, laughing or crying or both, which was the same thing and always had been.

On the sideline, Declan stood. Notebook in hand. Pen in his right fist. Still watching. Always watching.

The notebook's final entry would be made later, in the quiet of the dressing room. For now, one thought:

It works, Ciara, it works!

Six minutes of normal time plus whatever the referee added. Carrickmore threw everything forward: ten men, nine of them pushing into the Ballymore half, the goalkeeper on the edge of his box, screaming instructions that nobody was following.

Ballymore defended. Methodically. The right player in the right position at the right time, every time, because somebody was talking and somebody was listening and the system worked.

Minute eighty-seven: Carrickmore corner. Swinging in from the right. Every player in the box. Shay met it with a header that cleared the six-yard line and found Ciarán, who controlled it, held it, and ran toward the corner flag. Not to score, not to attack, but to let the clock run, and force the opposition to foul you or let time pass. Game Management. Play Five.

Ciarán held the ball for eleven seconds. It doesn't sound like much but in that match, eleven seconds was an eternity. The crowd counted. The referee watched. A Carrickmore midfielder lunged, and the ball went out for a throw-in to Ballymore, which was the same as possession, which was the same as time, which was the same as survival.

Minute eighty-nine: free kick to Carrickmore. Twenty-five metres out, central. Conor Fitzpatrick territory: his range, his angle, his trademark. The wall lined up. Kev positioned himself. The crowd held its breath.

Conor struck it. The technique was *perfect*: over the wall, dipping, heading for the top corner. But Kev was already there. The video analysis that Niamh had compiled and Declan had studied, showing him exactly where Conor aimed from this distance: top right, every time. Kev pushed it over the bar.

Ninety minutes. The board went up. Three minutes of added time.

Minute ninety-one: corner to Carrickmore. Shay headed clear. The ball went to Ciarán. Ciarán played it long, toward the Carrickmore half, where nobody was standing because every Carrickmore player was in the Ballymore box. The ball bounced once, twice, and rolled to a stop near the centre circle. A Carrickmore player had to sprint sixty metres to retrieve it. Clock ticking.

Minute ninety-two: cross from the right. High, hopeful, searching. Kev came off his line, a brave decision, the ball dropping in the zone between goalkeeper and defender where catastrophe lives. He punched it. The ball spun off his fist and landed twenty metres away, where a Carrickmore midfielder was waiting. Shot. Thirty metres. Rising. Over the bar.

The crowd groaned, then cheered, because the ball was over the bar and the ball over the bar was the ball not in the net.

Ninety-two minutes and forty seconds. Goal kick to Ballymore.

Kev placed the ball, stretching time, watching the referee. The referee was looking at his watch. Kev took the goal kick. Long. High. Into the Carrickmore half. The ball was in the air when the whistle blew.

Three blasts. Long. Short. Long. The universal signal that something is over.

Ballymore 4, Carrickmore 3.

The First Red

Chapter 17: After the Whistle

"The First Red is never on the pitch."

Fr. Tommy Walsh was standing on the grass bank when the whistle went.

He had been standing in the same spot for the entire second half, unable to sit, unable to move, his hands clasped in front of him in a posture that was indistinguishable from prayer and may, on several occasions, have been exactly that. He wore his parish jacket and his Ballymore scarf, and his glasses were fogged with the moisture that had been hanging in the air all afternoon, giving the final minutes of the match a soft-focus quality that he would later describe as "cinematic" and that was actually just condensation.

He watched his boys collapse onto each other on the pitch. And they were his boys; he'd christened eight of them, buried the grandparents of three others, and counselled Rory through the worst year of his life with tea and silence and a patience rooted in the fundamental belief that people are capable of change.

He watched Declan stand motionless on the sideline.

He watched the crowd pour down the grass bank in a tide of joy that had no particular direction and didn't need one.

And then Fr. Tommy Walsh, who had never been heard to use language stronger than "blast" in thirty-two years of ministry, who had survived parish council meetings and diocesan audits and the annual Christmas pageant without once losing his composure, turned to Paddy Joe Regan standing beside him with tears running openly down his face and both arms raised as though signalling the arrival of a helicopter or a miracle and said, with absolute clarity:

"Well, ride me sideways, Paddy Joe. We won. We won!"

Paddy Joe stared at him. His arms slowly lowered. His mouth opened. His tears, remarkably, stopped.

"Father?"

"You heard me."

A pause in which stories about the parish priest were born, ready to be shared over pints and coffees for the next twenty years.

"But don't tell the Bishop."

On the pitch, the celebrations had the quality of controlled chaos: people running in different directions with the same purpose, which was to find someone to hold and something to shout, not necessarily in that order.

Rory was sitting on the grass. He hadn't been able to stand since the final whistle: his legs had simply stopped, like a machine that had been running past its tolerance for forty minutes and had finally, gently, shut down. He sat with his knees up, his head back, looking at the grey sky, and let the noise wash over him.

Shay found him. Walked through the crowd, through the teammates, through the chaos, directly to Rory. He didn't say anything. He pulled Rory to his feet and held him, one arm around his shoulders. The grip was firm and warm and said everything that words couldn't:

I'm proud of you. You did it. You chose right.

Rory leaned into him. Two men on a football pitch in the rain, neither speaking.

Ciarán was somewhere underneath a pile of teammates. From the bottom of it, his voice: "Get off me, lads, you're crushing my ribs."

Damo was crying. Open, face-crumpled, shoulder-shaking. He was being held by two teammates and a stranger from the grass bank who had climbed the rope line without any clear authorisation.

Niamh found her father on the sideline. He was standing where he'd stood for ninety minutes, notebook in his left hand, pen in his right, collar up against the rain. His face was wet, and it might have been the rain and it might not have been.

She hugged him. He hugged her back with one arm. The notebook arm.

"Da. You did it."

"They did it."

"Da."

"I watched. That's all I did. I watched, and I told them what I saw, and they decided what to do about it."

"That's not all you did."

He looked at her. Nineteen years old. His daughter. Running water bottles and typing up notebook entries at midnight and standing on a sideline in the rain because she believed in what he believed in.

"No," he said. "I guess not."

He opened the notebook. Wrote the final entry:

Blues: 16. Reds: 0.

Below it, in the same pen, without pause:

It works.

The Carrickmore bus left at half five. Tinted windows up, Larkfield Holdings logo catching the low light, engine running while the last of the players climbed aboard. They moved through Paddy Joe's makeshift car park, with its cattle trailer and its 1997 Corolla in silence. Through the windows, if you looked, you could see eleven men sitting separately, headphones on, staring at phone screens, each processing the defeat alone because they had no shared language for processing it together.

Graham Welsh didn't get on the bus.

He sat on the bench long after the final whistle. The pitch was emptying. The grass bank was bare. The burger van was packing up, Tommy Flanagan counting his take, which had been extraordinary, because a thousand people with heightened emotions buy more burgers than eighty-seven people with moderate expectations, and he was already thinking about coming back for the third round.

The community centre lights were on. Inside, the sound of Ballymore's celebration, and what a celebration.

Roberta sat down beside him. She'd come down from the stand. Her laptop was closed. Her phone was in her pocket. She looked tired. The tiredness of a person who had been right about something and been ignored.

A long silence. Neither of them had the words yet.

"I showed them the data, Graham."

"I know."

"The cohesion report. The behavioural indicators. The risk assessment. I showed them everything."

"I know."

"They didn't look. They chose not to look."

"I know."

Another silence. Longer than the first. On the pitch, the groundskeeper was collecting corner flags.

"What would you do differently?" Roberta asked.

Graham looked at the pitch. At the goalposts. At the grass bank where a thousand people had stood and believed in something that the analytics dashboard said was impossible.

"Everything above the pitch," he said. "Nothing on it."

"Meaning?"

"Meaning the players were good enough. The coaching plan was there. The talent was there. The scouting was sound. Everything below the boardroom was fine."

He paused.

"The problem was everything above. The decisions I wasn't allowed to make. The culture I wasn't allowed to build. The trust I was never given. I couldn't change the defensive structure because the chairman vetoed it from a stand on a phone. I couldn't manage the substitutions because the chairman ordered them from a walkie-talkie. I couldn't resolve the conflict between Rourke and the left-back because the chairman said senior players manage themselves."

He turned to Roberta.

"And one other thing: I chose to accept it." He paused and gestured round him. "They earnt that win. Our skills and talent should have crushed them but they built a team, they saw our weakness, exploited it and let us defeat ourselves."

"And you think that was it? The difference?"

"Yes, basically. He was allowed to coach. He was allowed to make decisions based on what he saw, not what a committee approved. He was allowed to build a culture instead of managing a structure. He was allowed to prioritise behaviour over dashboard metrics. He had permission to lead."

Roberta thought about this.

"And you didn't."

"I had a budget. I had resources. I had the best players in the division. I had everything I needed except permission."

He paused and then looked at her again. "It's not just me, Roberta, it's the whole rotten system. All of us staring at dashboards and missing what was in front of our noses. And you knew too: you had the data, you had the insights and when they didn't listen, what should you do differently?"

Later, in the car park, Graham found Declan loading gear into a van that was older than several of the Ballymore players and had a Ballyboden St. Enda's sticker on the back window that was slowly peeling off.

The car park was almost empty. The celebration had moved inside. Through the community centre windows, the shadows of people dancing were visible against the light.

"That wasn't luck."

Declan looked up. Set down the kit bag.

"No."

"That was ... brilliant. What I saw today — the communication, the composure, the way they responded to conceding — that doesn't happen by accident."

"No."

"What did you see that we didn't?"

Declan leaned against the van. Looked at Graham the way he looked at a pitch — not with judgment, but with the calm, observational attention of a man who watched things carefully and drew conclusions slowly.

"But you did see it, Graham, I know you did. The right-back switching off. Your nine ignoring the runner. Communication breaking down."

"How do you—"

"Because you're a good coach. You see what I see. Difference is I was able to do something about it."

Silence.

"I tried to change the setup for today," Graham said. "Devlin overruled me. From the stand."

"Yes. That's a Red."

"A what?"

"A behavioural signal. Predicts what's coming. When a chairman overrules a coach during a match based on a dashboard instead of the pitch — that's not just a Red. That's the First Red. The one at the top. Makes all the others inevitable."

Graham stared at him.

"The First Red is never on the pitch." Declan added. "It's with whoever decides how much permission the people below them get. Your players were more than capable enough. Your coaching plan was good. The training was excellent. Everything was there for victory but the system above you strangled it."

Graham looked toward the community centre. Light, shadows, music.

"Can it be fixed?"

"Always. But only by those who make the decisions, not from the middle."

Silence.

"They were bloody good today your lads."

"Yes. They were."

DECLAN'S NOTEBOOK – Final page

Ballymore Utd 4 - 3 Carrickmore

FAI Cup, Second Round

BALLYMORE

Reds: 0

Blues:

○○○○○○○○○○○○
○○○○ (16)

CARRICKMORE

Reds:

●●●●●●●●●● (12+)

Blues:

○ (1)

Outcome = Capability × Behaviour

Them: 9 × 0.3 = 2.7

Us: 5 × 0.8 = 4.0

Just enough.

"The First Red is never on the pitch."

Roy Cullen was not a happy man. Carrickmore Town had lost humiliatingly to Ballymore United. He was down one hundred and fifty *thousand* euro. And somehow, that gobshite Mickey Brennan was at the bottom of it all. He didn't know how exactly but the whole incident had Mickey's greasy fingerprints all over it.

His betting shop was quiet when Declan walked in on Monday, the only customers a couple of elderly men studying form for Leopardstown.

Roy was behind the counter. "A hundred and fifty thousand," he said sourly, squinting in suspicion at the biggest winner he'd ever had to pay out. "I can't pay that amount out in cash, so I'll need bank account and ID and I'll transfer electronically."

Declan nodded. "I'd like four thousand in cash."

"Party time is it?"

"No, I just need to buy something."

Roy counted out four thousand euro in fifty-euro notes and placed it on the counter between them. The growing pile sat there, fat and significant, looking exactly like what it was: the financial proof of a mathematical model built on coloured pens and dice and the conviction that the thing nobody else was measuring was the thing that mattered most.

"You knew," Roy said. "How did you know they'd win?"

"I didn't know we'd win."

"You knew enough to bet nearly four grand."

"I knew the behaviours I'd seen from both teams made it possible. My model said thirty-six in a hundred, fifty-four in a hundred if we played the behaviours right. You priced us at two and a half in a hundred. That gap was the bet. Not the result. The gap."

"Behaviours!" Roy nearly spat the word out. "That's not an answer."

"It's the only honest one I can give you. I didn't know we'd win but I knew we could. I knew enough to know that betting on us, at those odds, was the right decision regardless of the outcome. That's what probabilistic thinking means. The data made it a good bet. Your odds made it a rational one. The day made it a winning one." Declan was on his soap box and lecturing, knew it and didn't care: he figured he'd earned the right to lecture a bit.

He took the envelope. It was heavier than he expected, or maybe it was exactly as heavy as he expected and the weight was something else, the weight of a conviction validated, of a risk taken and rewarded, of a man who had spent so many lonely years watching things nobody else watched and had been vindicated.

He bought back his car that afternoon. Got a lift from Rory. Paddy Joe's nephew tried to charge him retail until he saw the look on Rory's face and suddenly remembered how recently it had been sold and that he hadn't actually had time to do any preparation work on it yet now that he thought about it and sold it back to him for the purchase price. He drove straight to the pawnbrokers to purchase back the rings. His mother's ring went straight back in its box. The other, he slipped back on to his finger.

That evening in his kitchen, he sat down alone. Niamh had had to go back to college that morning and the kitchen table still had the brown paper from Aoife's Monte Carlo simulation, the probability curves and tally marks and coloured zones that had told him thirty-six in a hundred was enough to bet on. He should have cleared it away but he hadn't. It was proof that this had all happened and he didn't want to lose it yet.

He managed to retrieve his laptop from under the simulation and opened it, reflexively checking the website more from habit than hope. There was one new enquiry on the IMIRT website. The website was basic, three pages, a contact form, and a tagline that read "Work is a sport. Play to win." It had been built by Niamh in an afternoon using a template that cost twelve euros, and it received, on average, one enquiry per month, usually from someone who had mistyped an address looking for an immigration lawyer.

This one was different.

From: Roberta.Berbenni@larkfieldholdings.ie

I work for an organisation that measures everything and sees nothing. I think you measure the things that actually matter and see the signal. Can we talk?

He read it twice. Closed the laptop. Sat back.

Opened a fresh notebook.

The old one, the one that had seen eight weeks of training, a Monte Carlo simulation, and an FAI Cup match that nobody expected and nobody would forget, was full. Every page. Red dots, blue circles, green ticks, margin notes, probability calculations, and a final entry that said *Blues: 16. Reds: 0. It works.*

The new notebook was clean. Off-white pages. Spiral-bound. The cover would be lost to rain and use within a month. He picked up a red pen, because you always start with the Reds, and wrote:

"Behaviours are leading indicators."

Below it:

“The scoreboard is the last thing to change.”

Below that, after a pause:

“But the First Red is never on the pitch. It’s in the boardroom.”

He looked at the words. Looked at the email. Looked at the brown paper on his kitchen table, covered in Aoife’s handwriting and the mathematical proof of something he’d known to be true for so long.

Then he turned to the laptop again, and began to type a reply.

EPILOGUE: A Fresh Notebook

"What do you measure that tells you what's about to happen?"

Six months later in a boardroom in Dublin's financial district. Twelve executives with open-collar shirts and smart watches.

Declan stood at a whiteboard wearing Shay's jacket (slightly too big). Three people were checking phones. One was typing. Two were having a side conversation. He picked up his notebook and turned to a new page. Red, Red, Red.

"I want to tell you three stories," he said.

He told them about a penalty taker whose body language predicted the miss. About the GAA team that discovered that three turnovers predicted the match outcome 91% of the time. And finally about an amateur team that beat professionals by behaving like a team when the professionals behaved like individuals.

He wrote:

Outcome = Capability × Behaviour

"Your capability is a nine. Good engineers, good tools, funding. Nine."

He wrote: 9 × 0.3 = 2.7

“Behaviour multiplier of 0.3. Management overruling the people closest to the work. Conflicts unresolved. Everything priority number one. So we get nine times 0.3.”

He wrote: 5 × 0.8 = 4.0

“Less capable team. Better behaviours. They win.”

He looked at the VP of Engineering.

“Not five minutes ago, I was present here in this meeting and three of you were checking your phones, another typing, some side conversations. Those are all Reds. You were all here but none of you were present. There was no Focus.” A pause to let that sink in. “When was the last time everything in your organisation was priority number one?”

Uncomfortable laughter.

“That’s a Red. I’ll bet it showed up weeks before your last missed deadline but you didn’t see it because you weren’t watching for it.”

He wrote the fractal equation:

> **Outcome = Capability × Team Behaviours × Coaching Behaviours × Management Behaviours**

“Every layer multiplies. The First Red is never in the engineering team. It’s in this room.”

He capped the marker.

Karen Foley: "How do we start?"

Declan wrote:

WHAT DO YOU CONTROL?

"If the answer is 'everything,' that's your First Red."

He drove home. Jetta rattling, window whistling.

Ciarán called. "Rory's been offered a trial. League of Ireland. First Division."

Declan was quiet.

"He wants to talk to you first."

"Tell him to call me."

"And Dec? Shay wants his jacket back."

Finally home at the bungalow on the Ardmore Road. Gate still unpainted. Hedge still overgrown. But there was a signed consultancy contract on the counter from Larkfield Holdings. Devlin, it turned out, did not hold grudges when there was value to be had, and if there was one thing he understood, it was *capability*. And there were three new promising leads on the IMIRT website and that on top of the consultancy job with the bank today. He'd have to buy his own jacket soon.

Declan sat at the kitchen table. Roy Cullen had turned out to be as good as his word: a hundred and fifty thousand euros had been paid out, four thousand in cash, one hundred and forty-six thousand by bank transfer. Enough to clear every debt, fix the house up and put the rest away for Niamh so she'd never have to pawn her last possessions.

He put the kettle on, made a cup of tea and sat down.

"Well done, Dec. That's Niamh's future safe, right there."

"It was your doing, my love."

"How so? I've not been the one obsessing over watching people NOT play football for nine years!"

"Don't you remember, Ciara? You said it to me at that match, just before ... you know."

"Oh, I remember now. I said, 'You just know what they're going to do from the way they're standing, Dec.' And you just stared at me and asked what I meant and I said ..."

He cut in, because he knew every word: "'Well, look at that fella there now. Hasn't said a word to the fella next to him all match. And then they let that stupid goal from the other lot through. Wouldn't have happened if they'd just worked together now would it? Dec, you can *see* what's going to happen just from the way they're behaving.'"

And he'd stared at her even longer.

"What are you about there, Dec? You've always known I've witchcraft! Away with you!"

Almost the last words she'd ever said to him. But she'd been right. She had witchcraft and she'd been right and now he'd proved it.

Ciara was right and Niamh was safe and life could start again.

The End

APPENDICES

Appendix A: The Equation

Outcome = Capabilities × Behaviours

Most organisations spend their time and money on capabilities. Better tools, more training, bigger budgets, shinier technology. Fair enough. You need capabilities. But capabilities are only half the equation.

Behaviours are the other half. How people communicate, how they handle pressure, whether they collaborate or compete, whether conflicts get resolved or fester. And here's the thing that matters: the equation is multiplicative.

Not additive. Multiplicative. The distinction is everything.

If it were additive (Capability + Behaviour), bad behaviour would just knock a few points off the total. A team scoring 9 for capability and 2 for behaviour gets 11. Mediocre but survivable.

But it's multiplicative (Capability × Behaviour). So that same team scores 18 out of a possible 81. And a scrappier team with 5 capability and 8 behaviour scores 40. The scrappier team wins by a factor of two.

This is why organisations with vast resources get outperformed by smaller teams that work well together. Carrickmore had a 9 in capability. Their behaviour multiplier was closer to 0.3. Ballymore's capability was a 5. Their multiplier was 0.8. Do the maths.

It's Fractal

The equation doesn't stop at team level. It stacks:

> Outcome = Capability × Team Behaviours × Coaching Behaviours × Management Behaviours

Each layer multiplies the one below. Carrickmore's management (0.3) constrained their coaching (0.6), which capped their team behaviour (0.5), applied to capability (9). Effective performance: **0.81**. Ballymore: 0.9 × 0.9 × 0.8 × 5 = **3.24**.

You can't coach your way out of a management culture that won't let you coach.

Behaviours Predict

Capabilities tell you what's possible. Outcomes tell you what happened. Behaviours tell you what's *about to happen*.

Declan bet on the match because the behaviours told a different story from the bookmaker's odds. Not because he knew Ballymore would win. He didn't. They had a 36% chance. But the market priced them at 3%. That gap between what the behaviours showed and what the market believed was worth betting on, regardless of the result.

In your organisation: when communication drops, when conflicts go unresolved, when everything becomes priority one, those aren't symptoms. They're forecasts. They show up weeks before the missed deadlines.

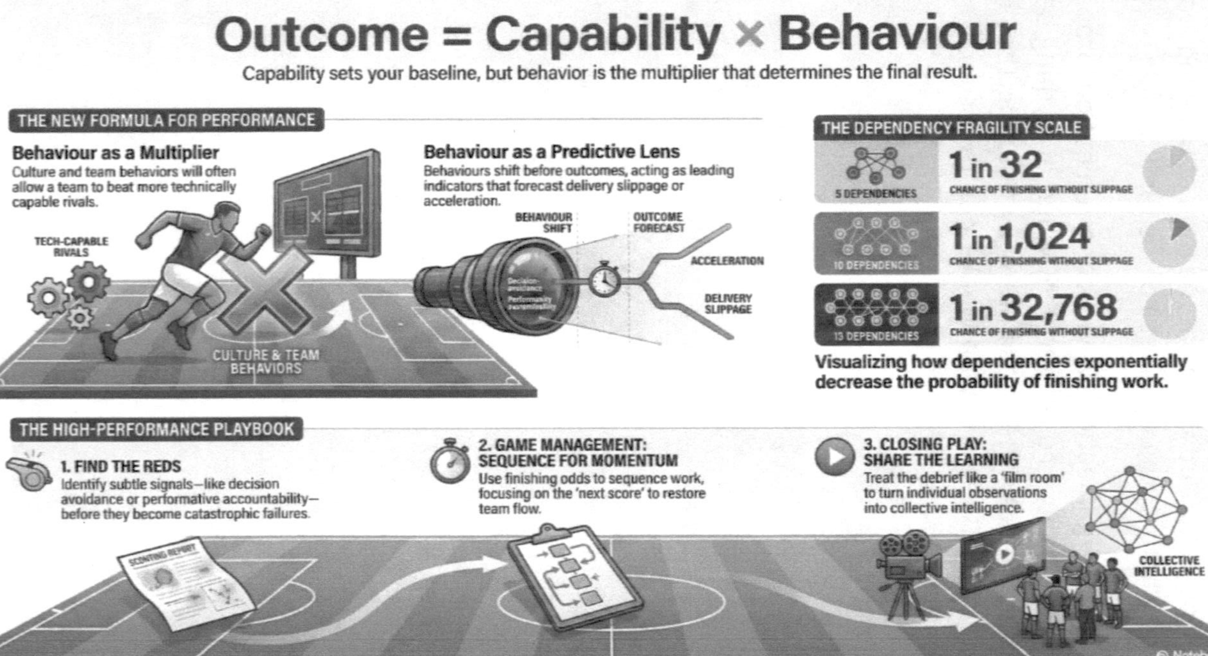
Outcome = Capability × Behaviour
Capability sets your baseline, but behavior is the multiplier that determines the final result.
THE NEW FORMULA FOR PERFORMANCE
Behaviour as a Multiplier
Culture and team behaviors will often allow a team to beat more technically capable rivals.
TECH-CAPABLE RIVALS
CULTURE & TEAM BEHAVIORS
Behaviour as a Predictive Lens
Behaviours shift before outcomes, acting as leading indicators that forecast delivery slippage or acceleration.
BEHAVIOUR SHIFT
OUTCOME FORECAST
ACCELERATION
DELIVERY SLIPPAGE
THE DEPENDENCY FRAGILITY SCALE
5 DEPENDENCIES
1 in 32
CHANCE OF FINISHING WITHOUT SLIPPAGE
10 DEPENDENCIES
1 in 1,024
CHANCE OF FINISHING WITHOUT SLIPPAGE
13 DEPENDENCIES
1 in 32,768
CHANCE OF FINISHING WITHOUT SLIPPAGE
Visualizing how dependencies exponentially decrease the probability of finishing work.
THE HIGH-PERFORMANCE PLAYBOOK
1. FIND THE REDS
Identify subtle signals—like decision avoidance or performative accountability—before they become catastrophic failures.
SCOUTING REPORT
2. GAME MANAGEMENT: SEQUENCE FOR MOMENTUM
Use finishing odds to sequence work, focusing on the 'next score' to restore team flow.
3. CLOSING PLAY: SHARE THE LEARNING
Treat the debrief like a 'film room' to turn individual observations into collective intelligence.
COLLECTIVE INTELLIGENCE
NotebookLM

Appendix B: The Five Plays — A Practical Guide

Play 1: FOCUS

What it is: The discipline of prioritising one thing at a time.

Observable behaviours (Blues):

- Team can articulate the current priority in five words or fewer
- Work in progress is limited
- When new requests arrive, the team asks “does this replace or add?”

The First Red: When everything becomes priority number one.

How to start: At your next team meeting, ask: “What is the single most important thing we need to finish this week?” If the answer contains more than one thing, you’ve found your Red.

Play 2: SEE THE PITCH

What it is: Creating visibility of the whole system, not just your own work.

Observable behaviours (Blues):

- Team members can describe what others are working on
- Work is visualised to show flow, not just status
- Information flows laterally, not just vertically

How to start: Record your standup. Watch it back. How much is about individual tasks vs connections between tasks?

Play 3: FIND THE REDS

What it is: Watching for behavioural signals that predict negative outcomes.

Observable Behaviours (Reds):

- Communication frequency dropping
- Response time to problems increasing
- Conflicts going unresolved
- Blame language increasing
- The "everything is priority one" signal

How to start: For two weeks, keep a notebook. After every meeting, note Reds and Blues. Try and find at least one of each but don't force it. After two weeks, look for patterns.

Play 4: STACK THE ODDS

What it is: Making decisions based on probability. Choosing the high-probability option and keeping dependency-chains small, tight and necessary.

Observable behaviours (Blues):

- Teams prioritise by likelihood of completion, not just value
- Dependencies are minimised before work starts
- Simple approaches preferred over novel ones

How to start: For your next planning session, ask for every item: “What are the odds this gets finished?” Sequence by probability, highest first.

Play 5: GAME MANAGEMENT

What it is: Controlling tempo and maintaining composure under pressure.

Observable behaviours (Blues):

- Teams respond to setbacks with calm reorganisation
- Tempo is deliberate: pressure increases, team slows down to think
- Leaders model composure

How to start: Next time something goes wrong, watch the first sixty seconds. Who speaks? What do they say? Does the team organise or scatter? Those sixty seconds tell you more than any engagement survey.

Appendix C: Declan's Notebook — A Reader's Guide

What You Need

- A small notebook
- A red pen, a blue pen, and a green pen
- The willingness to watch behaviours instead of activities

How to Use It

During any interaction, watch for:

REDS ● — Mark a red dot when you observe:

- Someone disengages (phone, laptop, eyes glazing)
- A question goes unanswered
- Conflict is avoided or escalated rather than resolved
- Someone is blamed publicly
- "Everything is a priority"

BLUES ○ — Mark a blue dot when you observe:

- Someone proactively communicates without being asked

- A mistake is owned honestly
- Two people resolve a disagreement directly
- Someone asks a question that changes the conversation
- A team member helps another without being asked

GREENS ✓ — Competent but unremarkable. Necessary but not predictive.

The Three-Red Rule

Three or more Reds in a single interaction predicted negative outcomes 91% of the time in Declan's data. Track this threshold to start and modify as necessary.

Appendix D: The Forecast — Monte Carlo in Five Minutes

The Principle

Instead of a binary question like "will we hit this deadline?" or "Will we win?", ask "what's the probability?" Then run scenarios.

This gives you a range of outcomes with associated risks.

Monte Carlo in Practice

Aoife didn't predict the result. She mapped the range of possible results and asked how often Ballymore won.

That's Monte Carlo simulation: run the scenario a thousand times with realistic variation, then count the outcomes. It doesn't tell you what will happen. It tells you what could happen, and how often.

How it works:

1. Define your variables (capability scores, behaviour multipliers)
2. Add realistic variation to each (not every match plays out identically)

3. Calculate the outcome for one simulated match
4. Repeat 1,000 times
5. Count: how often does Team A win?

Aoife did this with dice on brown paper. You can do it in ten lines of Python (which would have been a more practical solution for Aoife but less interesting in the story):

```
import random
wins = 0
for _ in range(10000):
 # Ballymore: capability 5, behaviour 0.6-1.0
 ballymore = 5 * random.uniform(0.6, 1.0)
 # Carrickmore: capability 9, behaviour 0.1-0.5
 carrickmore = 9 * random.uniform(0.1, 0.5)
 if ballymore > carrickmore:
  wins += 1

print(f"Ballymore wins: {wins/100:.1f}%")
```

Run it. Change the ranges. See what happens when Carrickmore's behaviour improves. See what happens when Ballymore's drops. The numbers move. That's the point — behaviours change the probability before the outcome arrives.

The market priced Ballymore at 2.5%. The simulation said 36%. The gap was the opportunity. It was neither certainty nor prediction but a range of outcomes with realistic probabilities.

Appendix E: The Bookshelf

What Declan reads, a sample:

David Marquet — *Turn the Ship Around!* Push decision-making to where the information lives. Declan's entire philosophy — teaching players to read the game rather than follow instructions — comes from Marquet.

Gene Kim et al. — *The Phoenix Project* The original business novel proving systems thinking can be taught through fiction.

General McChrystal — *Team of Teams* Shared consciousness. Small teams connected by trust and real-time information.

Michael Lewis — *Moneyball* The market prices the wrong things. Someone who prices the right things can win with less.

Eliyahu Goldratt — *The Goal* The constraint is never where you think. The bottleneck is at the top of the bottle.

Annie Duke — *Thinking in Bets* Decision quality and outcome quality are different. The data made it a good bet regardless of the result.

James Kerr — *Legacy* The All Blacks. Sweep the sheds. Shay's behaviour — arriving first, folding jerseys — is Legacy in action.

Daniel Coyle — *The Culture Code* Safety, vulnerability, purpose. Ballymore has all three. Carrickmore has none.

James Clear — *Atomic Habits* Behaviours compound. Tiny improvements in communication and composure that add up to a transformed team.

Appendix F: About IMIRT

IMIRT (pronounced "im-erch") is an Irish word meaning "play" or "sport" from the verb *imir*. It seemed the right name for something built on the conviction that the principles which make teams perform in sport are the same principles that make teams perform at work and hence the website: https://www.imirt.work. You can contact us for real via the website, although it won't be Declan himself responding.

The five plays in this book are real. They came from many years of watching what actually predicts performance, in football and in business, and finding that the answer was almost never what people expected.

If this book made you look differently at how your own team behaves, that's the start. The equation works the same way whether the pitch is grass or carpet tile.

https://www.imirt.work

About the Author

Andrew Locatelli Woodcock has spent over twenty years leading software engineering teams at organisations including Citibank, UL Inc, PTC, ESW, and others, growing teams of up to 110 engineers across multiple sites including Dublin and Madrid. The same question followed him through every role: why do talented teams underperform?

The answer was never capability. It was behaviour — the signals visible in how people communicate, make decisions, and respond under pressure. The IMIRT framework grew out of discussions with a work colleague, Kieran Neeson, now co-founder of IMIRT, for tracking those signals and predicting delivery outcomes before they happened. The First Red is the story of what happens when you hand that system to a retired coach with a notebook and a point to prove.

Andrew lives in Dublin, Ireland.

www.ingramcontent.com/pod-product-compliance
Lightning Source LLC
LaVergne TN
LVHW091127080826
845145LV00008B/2073